THE PERFECTLY IMPERFECT Proverbs 31 WOMAN

TARA BEATTIE

The Perfectly Imperfect Proverbs 31 Woman
Trilogy Christian Publishers
A Wholly Owned Subsidiary of Trinity Broadcasting Network
2442 Michelle Drive
Tustin, CA 92780
Copyright © 2021 by Tara Beattie
Scripture quotations marked NASB are taken from the New American Standard Bible® (NASB), Copyright © 1960, 1962, 1963, 1968, 1971, 1972, 1973, 1975, 1977, 1995 by The Lockman Foundation. Used by permission. www.Lockman.org.
Scripture quotations marked ESV are from The Holy Bible, English Standard Version®, copyright © 2001 by Crossway, a publishing ministry of Good News Publishers. Used by permission. All rights reserved.
All Scripture quotations marked NIV are taken from THE HOLY BIBLE, NEW INTERNATIONAL VERSION®, NIV® Copyright © 1973, 1978, 1984, 2011 by Biblica, Inc.® Used by permission. All rights reserved worldwide.
Scriptures marked NKJV are taken from the NEW KING JAMES VERSION®. Copyright© 1982 by Thomas Nelson, Inc. Used by permission. All rights reserved.
All rights reserved, including the right to reproduce this book or portions thereof in any form whatsoever.
For information, address Trilogy Christian Publishing
Rights Department, 2442 Michelle Drive, Tustin, Ca 92780.
Trilogy Christian Publishing/ TBN and colophon are trademarks of Trinity Broadcasting Network.
For information about special discounts for bulk purchases, please contact Trilogy Christian Publishing.
Manufactured in the United States of America
Trilogy Disclaimer: The views and content expressed in this book are those of the author and may not necessarily reflect the views and doctrine of Trilogy Christian Publishing or the Trinity Broadcasting Network.

10 9 8 7 6 5 4 3 2 1
Library of Congress Cataloging-in-Publication Data is available.
ISBN: 978-1-63769-882-2
ISBN: 978-1-63769-883-9

Dedication:

This book is dedicated to all the women out there who are struggling with fear, anxiety, past hurts, anger, and feeling like they are not enough. Sweet sisters, look up and listen up, YOU ARE ENOUGH. You have been perfectly and wonderfully made by God for a time such as this. You are the daughters of The King. Through Jesus, we have faith and hope. We have love from a Father that we cannot even begin to fathom that type of love. We have a sisterhood of fellow believers who are as fierce as mama lions when it comes to being prayer warriors. There is this unexplainable joy that comes from a personal relationship with Jesus.

I know you. I was you. I know your hurts, your anger, your anxiety, and your fears. I know your heart and I know that this is not easy, but I also know that allowing God in allowed me to fully begin healing. Life is much better when I step back and allow Jesus in the driver's seat. Here is my plea to you, give it a shot and join me on this adventure in growing a deeper relationship with Jesus. What do you have to lose? You have eternity to gain.

Endorsements:

"Tara has a God given gift in showing her heart for Jesus in her writing. From the beginning You will feel drawn to a life giving and loving Savior."

- Pastor Bo Gerken at Living Proof Church in Paola, KS

The Perfectly Imperfect Proverbs 31 Woman by Tara Beattie is for all of us out there in this big, messed up world that love Jesus. This book is filled with hope, encouragement, and true testimonies from an imperfect woman that lives to grow her relationship with God closer every day. I know I am flawed and not perfect, but it is a promising feeling I now have, knowing other women share similar flaws and stories as myself. If you are just beginning your walk with Jesus or haven't even started your walk yet, this book is a must-read!

-Angela Wilcox, friend of Tara's, neighbor lady, almost professional Tik-Tok-er, Teacher to the Youth of America, an imperfect lady who loves Jesus

Foreword:

Written by Glenda Bunkofske and Rosemary Johnson.

As I read through the pages of *The Perfectly Imperfect Proverbs 31 Woman*, I found myself smiling, laughing, and crying. Many of the events and activities in this book, I remember. So, when she speaks of how much she loves her family and says she lives her life with authenticity- it is true. I have experienced and witnessed some of the events firsthand. She does live her life as she is and makes no apologies for living it with authenticity – that means when life is good and when life is bad. From Black Friday shopping in Branson, the tears of lost little ones, the conversations of what is this raising your hands in church about, to laughter at some silly event, it has been my pleasure to watch her grow as a woman of God. Tara is setting an example for her children, sister, friends, and family. Tara is standing strong in her love of God and her faith in his Word. I pray as you read this book, you can catch a glimpse of the fun-loving girl who has given her life over to God and learned it's okay to not be perfect.

— Glenda Bunkofske, better known as Aunt Glenda

It has been a blessing to watch Tara grow in her faith and stand on the Word of God as she moves through life—a life that is busy with being a devoted wife and mother, committed church member and lover of family and friends. I am happily looking forward to reading *The Perfectly Imperfect Proverbs 31 Woman*.

— Rose Mary Johnson, bett known as Grandma Rose

Preface:

I wanted to share my story to give other women hope and encouragement. I am a mess. On good days and bad days alike, I am a mess. But let me let you in on some good news, I am His mess. God is good and faithful all the time. We are not called to be perfect. As women, we are called to wear many hats such as wife, mom, cook, chauffeur, and dare I say, maid. We are called to press into the Father. At the end of the day, I want more to be more like Jesus and whole lot less of me. I love Jesus with all of my heart. I want to grow in my relationship with God each day. I want to give other women hope that I once so desperately needed. I want to see my kids grow in their relationship with God. Sister, I hope this book allows you the opportunity to grow in your faith. My fervent prayer is that you let the walls down and you let God take the wheel.

Who am I? I am someone who loves to poke fun at the most mundane things in life. I love to use humor in my everyday life. I love lattes especially vanilla with lavender. I will only drink hot lattes. I cannot even try a cold latte. I love my dog, Chloe. I love living in the country especially with all our sweet farm animals. I am not a city girl by no means. I love my family and friends like crazy. I love life.

And most important, I love who I have become when I quit running from Jesus and started running to Him.

Let me be clear, I did not write this book because I have it all together. I wrote this book because I do not have it all together. I am leaning on God's mercy and grace each and every day. It is through God's mercy and grace and never-ending love that I am getting through the day to day. I have come to the realization that I cannot do this thing called life on my own. I need a SAVIOR. We all need a Savior. The enemy is on full scale attack- all day, every day. The enemy does not care nor submit to the rules of a civil engagement of warfare. Their mission is simply and comes straight from scripture as we see in John 10:10, "The thief comes only to steal and kill and destroy," ah but then there is the King of King who sets the tone with the enemy, "I have come that they may have life, and have it to the full." It is a fact that the enemy will attack but it is of greater note that Good will defeat evil. As we go through this book together, we will discuss spiritual warfare and how the enemy is manipulative and deceptive, but we will also lean and press into God's promises from scripture. And the Good news is, well, we know how this story ends.

I have spent a year and half pouring my heart into this book. This is my testimony. This book is my love letter

PREFACE

to Jesus for never giving up on me, even when I ran away from Him and when I boxed Him in to fit my narrative. I am praying that this book becomes something that gives other hard-headed girls who are a mess...well, hope. Hope they are never too far gone for the Love of the Father. Freedom in fact that chains have been broken and the best is yet to come. I am praying that women realize that they are under spiritual warfare from the enemy and that praise, worship, scripture, and the Love of the Father are the methods to sending the enemy back where it came from. I am praying that women know it is okay to be vulnerable and that collectively we are called to surround each other in prayer and encouragement. I am hopeful that we can kick the comparison nonsense to the curb where it belongs. I hope someone finds encouragement that I am an absolute mess. I know for a fact that Jesus loves us hot mess girls just the same as he loves those who are not a hot mess.

Acknowledgements:

God! Thank you for guiding the writing of this book. Thank You for giving me the courage to share my heart with those reading. My prayer is that this book can stir the heart of at least one woman to turn her life to the Lord or establish a more meaningful relationship with God. With God's sweet grace this book is written for women who are desperately seeking God. This book is for women who do not have it all together but who seek God, who has it all together.

Without a doubt, my husband, Keith is sent straight from God. I am beyond grateful that God joined our hearts in marriage. I am grateful for you and your loving heart. I love doing life with you. Thank you for being you and always encouraging me along this path. Olive Juice. To my kids- Kinsley, Brody, and Brogan; thank you for your sweet inspiring words while I was writing this book. Thank you all for your understanding of my need for quiet time while writing, editing and praising God along this journey. I adore you all! I am ready for a week of cuddles, movies and lounging around the beach with you all. I love you guys so much!

My Aunt Glenda and Grandma Rose spent many years in prayer over me throughout the years. These two women are excellent examples of women who chase after Jesus.

They are not the type of women to turn to the world in times of adversity. They are women who press in deeper to the comfort and love of the Father. They are women of strength and absolute prayer warriors. From the very bottom of my heart, thank you! I love you two so very much!

Grandpa Leon, thank you for being a pillar in my life. I think the world of you. You have such an amazing character of strength and perseverance. You love unconditionally, and you never had to, that is what makes you even more amazing! You mean more to me than I will ever be able to capture in words. You are so much more than my grandpa; you are my encourager. I love you!

My Grandpa Keith and Grandma JoAnn, I really wish you were both here to be a part of our lives. Our family misses you both something fierce. You two were such a strong influence on me as I grew up. I truly had the very best grandparents. Grandpa, I am humbled by your life after Grandma passed away. You devoted your life to serving others. You served at your church. You served your community. You served your friends. You served without seeking any type of recognition. You taught me by example how to serve others well. I love you both! I will see you again!

Mom and Dad, thank you for loving me! Being a parent has taught me one thing, I am so sorry for any hurt or pain

I caused you and you were right, I was wrong (that hurts). I love you both with all that I am. I want nothing more than to stand beside you both on Sunday mornings. I am praying that God gets ahold of you both in a big way. Thank you for loving me when I was a difficult child and teen. We have seen great times and we have traveled through difficult times together but here we are together. I am grateful that God chose you both to be mine. You have been taught me the value of hard work and determination. Thank you for all your sacrifices as you raised Randall, Tiffany, and me, they did not go unnoticed. I love nothing more than hearing Kinsley, Brody and Brogan praying for you both. I will save a seat for you both on Sunday. Love you both!

Tiffany, I am grateful that God chose for us to be sisters. It is crazy how our spiritual walks line up and we both know it is totally a God-thing. To be able to pray with you as you accepted Jesus into your heart was one of the most pivotal moments in my life. It was that moment that solidified my journey to get to know Jesus on a deeper and more meaningful level. It is amazing to see how God has gotten ahold of you. I love you with all my heart!

Alicia- you are my person. You get me so well. She has been known to proofread my emails and tell her hot-headed friend to start over and not send the first draft- which is wise beyond words. I will never have the words to be able to capture how grateful I am for this special friendship. We have grown to be the very best of friends. You have encouraged me in so many ways. You do the most amazing job of reining me in when you need to which is often. I am sure Keith appreciates the help! I love that we get to do life together. We get to lean on each other as we venture through this journey called motherhood. Thank you for always being my person. I love you a latte. I love you beyond words. Thank you!

Carrie, I love you. I love that you have this amazing heart! You are one of my closest friends. I am beyond blessed by our friendship. Thank you for being someone I can be really real with. Maybe sometimes too real. Thank you for being some of our most dear friends and for the great conversation.

Angela, Shannon and Kelly. I love you girls! I love your families. Angela, I am grateful that you live just down the road. Thank you for encouraging "my walks with Jesus." We are so grateful to be able to do life with such an amazing family. Shannon- oh girl! I love your heart! You are a warrior and servant tied into one. You are an AMAZING mom. Thank you for having that home that my kids just want to hang out at. Let's go on vacation again. Like tomorrow. Kelly- Hey fellow VIKING! You have a heart of gold. See what I did there? Blue and Gold, you have to be a VIKING to get it. You are such a joy to be around. Um, did we become besties like overnight? You are my soul sister without a doubt. I love you all!

Ann, thank you for all you do for our family. You are always there to lend a helping hand. I am grateful for all you do. Thank you for loving and encouraging me. I am grateful that you are leading your family to follow Jesus by example. You exemplify the heart of a servant. I love you!

Susan, you are the best sister-in-law a girl could ask for. I love that we can share notes on the newest Jack Hibbs message. Thank you for the being the someone is dependable and loving. I love that you and Keith and I have gotten closer through our faith walks. Thank you! Love ya!

I wrote this book because of the outpour of support and love of my church fam. I never in a million years thought I would be involved in church and raising my family in the church. Living Proof is one of the greatest blessings in my life and the life of my family. Bo and Kristian- Thank You for everything! I do not think you guys hear thank you quite enough! Love ya both! My church family has encouraged and challenged me to pursue Jesus. I love seeing God move and move in a big way in our little community. Hey LP, the best is yet to come! Love you all!

Special shoutout to the Real Women of LP Facebook group. I want to be more intentional with my relationships, especially my relationships with other women. Sometimes I can be standoffish and stick to what is comfortable. Anyway, I love you all! As women we are called to love on each other well and be women on fire for God. Thank you all for touching my heart and being a part of this LP Women's Group that has been a blessing to many.

I am who I am because of the impacts that you have all made in my life- both those spoken aloud and in my heart. I am beyond words grateful and thankful. I love you all!

Introduction:

There are a few things that I know for certain. I am a self-professed hot mess most of the time. Usually, a funny hot mess, but a hot mess all the same. I like to poke fun at the mess that I am. Let's be honest, if I did not make fun of it, I would lose my mind. I am the mom that will burn the cinnamon rolls and then use a cheese grater to attempt to salvage those rolls all the while crying out that I will not let the enemy steal my joy and then tears immediately begin to flow due to ruined expectations I set for that morning's breakfast. I am certainly someone who has always liked things my way. I have been known to think that there are no other means or routes to do things other than the one mapped out by me. I still fight this battle. I find myself in battle with thinking I need to control the situation and the outcome. I can lose my mind when things fall short of the straight up ridiculous expectations that I have envisioned for a particular situation.

I am a hot mess. I am far from perfect though I have been seeking perfection in all aspects of life. I am a typical first born. I have been on a journey to find my place in life as a Christian woman who is desperately seeking her Savior. I began journaling as a form of healing from past hurts.

I decided to write this book to give all the hot mess mamas and ladies hope. I want other women to know that we are in this together. We aspire to be the Proverbs 31 Woman as sought out by King Lemuel and his mother. For the longest time, I did not read the passages regarding the Proverbs 31 Woman correctly. I pictured her as a woman who had it all together, never faltered and someone who commanded a room. I envisioned this woman to be without fault. I was wrong. These verses are simply trying to communicate what Lemuel should look for in a wife as a King. She would be someone who is a true partner to her husband and stands with him. She is a woman who is not running scared when it comes to doing the hard work and getting the job done. She is someone who does not shuck her responsibilities to her husband, family, or community. She also has to have the heart of a servant. She has the willingness and ability to look after her family. She does not lack confidence. After reading the verses about twenty-five times, I could not locate in the text where it states a wife should be perfect, or a woman should be perfect for that matter. The Proverbs 31 Woman set a precedent but does not require perfection.

I am constantly growing in who He wants me to be. Each day, I try to grow closer to God. I fail and I will continue to fail, but those failures do not define me. I am an

Introduction

Overcomer. I never thought it would be so easy and yet so hard at the same time to share my most intimate thoughts with you. Once I let God lead the writing of this book, I realized it is his grace and mercy that is flowing through me.

Table of Contents

Prologue 25

Chapter 1 My Reality: My Messy Life 29

Chapter 2 The Enemy 39

Chapter 3 Oh Goodness…I Am a Wife 47

Chapter 4 My Family 55

Chapter 5 My Hurts 63

Chapter 6 From Broken to Blessed 71

Chapter 7 A Forgiving Heart 81

Chapter 8 The Quirky Side of Things 87

Chapter 9 Cause Mommin' Ain't Easy 93

Chapter 10 Here Comes the

  Boom: Stress Overload 99

Chapter 11 I AM HIS: How to Be

  a Perfectly Imperfect

  Proverbs 31 Woman (Hot Mess) 105

Chapter 12 Worship 109

Chapter 13 Sweet Joy 119

Chapter 14 Her View on the World 125

Prologue:

I wrote this book after one of my favorite Bible verses, "The Proverbs 31 Woman." I began thinking about this so-called Proverbs 31 woman and instantly my mind went to this woman is perfection. How can a simpleton who burns cinnamon rolls on the regular ever live up to this calling? And that is how this journey began.

My mind instantly went to a place of perfection with the Proverbs 31 woman. It is sad but true. I am going to blame the fact that we live in a world that puts such a bounty on perfectionism. We see it every day via Pinterest, Fakebook, and Instagram. I will be honest that perfectionism is debilitating for me. The need to obtain perfection has left me with incomplete projects due to debilitating fear. As I wrote this book. I read and re-read Proverbs 31 and had a little newsflash moment when I learned those verses of scripture never mention the word perfect. Here is the Proverbs 31 Woman in a nutshell…she values her family, and her family is a top priority in her life. She does her husband good. She works hard and helps her family. She has the heart of a servant and serves others in her community well.

You see what happened there? I let the worldly way of life tell me what the Proverbs 31 Woman should be. I let the world set my expectations. Let's be honest, we are all mamas, grandmas, sisters, and friends who love Jesus but mess up on the daily. We fall short. I am one that has to find the humor in those mess ups, so those mess ups do not tear me to shreds. I mean who really thinks their teenagers are going to lick raw chicken or that they need to have a risk mitigation plan when visiting the zoo? Read on further it will all make sense soon enough. God has taken my mess and made me a messenger. I am excited to share my heart with you as we go on this journey of *The Perfectly Imperfect Proverbs 31 Woman* and how she just wants to drink lattes, serve, and love others all the while chasing after Jesus. Stay tuned sweet friends, the best is yet to come.

I used to believe in fairytales. I used to believe in the fantasy of happily ever after. I used to believe that I could handle all the things that life would throw at me on my own. I also used to think I was somewhat invincible. I lived my life in a manner that made me feel good. I did not really think there was another way to live. I dreamed of white picket fences, raising perfect kids, and living this seemingly perfect life. I am such an independent thinker that I actually thought I could do this on my own. Well, my life has been anything but perfect. I truly begin to dream and change my perspective on life when I quit trying to control everything and God took His rightful place in the driver's seat. Sweet friends, buckle in and let's take a little trip on how I finally reached the dream of becoming a Perfectly Imperfect Proverbs 31 Woman.

Chapter 1:

My Reality: My Messy Life

I always wanted everything to be perfect. All my life I have struggled with a distorted Disney view of what my life should look like. You know what I am talking about, that picture perfect scenario where everyone and everything looks like it is straight from a magazine cover. I remember being a young girl dreaming of this picture-perfect life. I planned to be a June Cleaver'esque wife and mother with that perfectly placed white picket fence. I have always had a weird infatuation with white picket fences. Oh, and I believed that I would have the most well-behaved children who are always flawlessly put together without a hair out of place. Almost like little robots. Well…I am calling crap on the whole idea of *PERFECTIONISM*. I am far from a June Cleaver'esque wife. If you ask my husband, he will laugh hysterically at the thought of June Cleaver and me even in the same sentence. Okay, I am not sure Keith has ever laughed hysterically at anything, but you get what I am saying…it is far -fetched. I am more like a combination of Susan Meyer from Desperate Housewives and her hair brained ideas meets a good ole controlling Claire Dunphy from Modern Family mixed with a little sarcasm and nonsense from American Housewives' Katie Otto topped off with the crazy antics of Clark W. Griswold, Jr. All these different personalities kind of create a trifecta of awesomeness if you will, or more accurately the perfect storm of a hot mess. I can certainly relate to Claire Dunphy in trying to find perfection in controlling all aspects of life. I channel Clark Griswold in the fact that I love my family fiercely and have all the best intentions and sometimes meet some hijinks along the way. I will be the first to say that I have been searching for "perfection" in almost everything under the sun. I wanted the "perfect wedding." Well, that did not happen. The unity candle melted, yes, you read that right, **the unity candle** melted in the trunk of my car the night before my late June wedding. Mass chaos ensued sending my parents to the local Wal-Mart for a generic unity candle. I can look back and smile about it now, but in the heat of the moment it caused me to slip into an irrational state of crazy-town that included an abundance of tears and the emergence of me as a Bridezilla. Thank goodness Bridezilla was short lived. I am thankful for sweet family and friends that talked me off the ledge. The good news is, everything worked out and we just celebrated eighteen (18) years of wedded bliss in June 2021. Stay tuned for more about "wedded bliss."

Um, no. The above sentence is not accurate. It has not been wedded bliss all the time. Some days early on in our marriage, I debated heading to Wal Mart to buy a cast iron skillet to help us "work through our problems." Just kidding. I did not even know what a cast iron skillet was. I was a terrible cook with a horrible temper who had issues letting anything go. I thought marriage was easy. I actually thought marriage was easy. Gosh, that hurts to even write those words. I struggled in the beginning. I was so set on being right that I did not even take my husband's feelings into account the majority of the time. It was the Tara show. I did not know how to fight fair. I did not realize you could disagree and it not be the end all. I think it is more than an appropriate time to say, "Keith- I am so sorry for being a complete jerk early on in our marriage. I am so beyond grateful that you had the love of Jesus in your heart to deal with me and my insane antics."

In complete delusional thinking, I expected a seamless balance as a working mom and wife. Still working on that one. Y'all I expected my kids to be these diligent little people, kind of like little robots who were always sweet and praised their mama with declarations of admiration. Oh, and they always had it together and *ACTUALLY* would want to keep their rooms clean and offer to clean up after themselves on their own. Uh ya, not so much. I envisioned completely unrealistic expectations for my family and myself. I held us to a standard that we can never achieve. We are fallible. We are human. I continue to struggle with setting realistic expectations in my life. I think this is something that I will always need to work to keep my expectations at an obtainable level.

Life is messy. Kids are messy. Husbands are certainly messy. The cars and house do not self-clean, well, at least not yet anyways! I have my moments which can sometimes go into days, where I just struggle with the mundane. I struggle with the fact that my kids are going to lose it from time to time or basically every day during Covid. Mamas, you are going to charbroil cinnamon rolls and then use the cheese grader to try and salvage them while your kids slowly walk away due to actual fear from a look of the caged beast once known as their sweet mama. True story there. I let that single moment turn into a whole day of epic disasters.

Ladies, your husband is going to fail you. They are far from perfect and surprise, surprise they have faults that seem to be on full display in the absolutely worst of times. We are going to fail our husbands. Bottom line is our contentment does not come from material things, places (I do love some Hobby Lobby) and it certainly does not come from the approval of others. Sweet friends, once we stop living for the approval of others the most amazing thing happens. We find a whole new level of peace. Our peace and contentment come from a personal relationship with God and constantly nurturing, growing, and pouring into that relationship.

For several years I was not putting God first. Let's be honest, I did not have a meaningful relationship with Christ. I had religion but no relationship. God was investing in a relationship with me, but it was purely one-sided. I was trapped in that circle of putting the world first. For a long time, I searched for perfection in my home, my children, my husband, and my job. I wanted perfection in worldly things. I was not investing in any type of relationship with God. I was in a personal battle with anger, bitterness, and carrying around a whole mess of resentment. I was desperately seeking the approval of everyone that I came in contact with as a result of living an unfulfilled life based on my own understanding and not pursuing a relationship with the Father.

It is only in recent months, that I have *finally* learned a hard life lesson. Listen very closely sweet friends, we are not defined through the opinions of other people, certain situations, or certain expectations, we find it through our faith in Jesus. Let's be real here, the only "perfect human" to ever walk this Earth is Jesus. And last I checked He still owned and always will be the only title holder of a perfect human.

I am no longer searching for the need to find perfection in everything and everyone. The only perfection that I want to pursue is a relationship with Jesus. I mean you ladies can relate, my house is lived in. On any given day, my house is somewhere between Pinterest worthy pictures or an episode of Hoarders with a side of a construction debris for that well-planned project that my darling husband started but has yet to finish…two years later. Sorry, not sorry, dear.

I love this simple verse in Philippians 3:12 (NAS) "Not that I have already obtained it or have already become perfect, but I press on so that I may lay hold of that for which also I was laid hold of by Christ Jesus."

This verse has taught me to press into Christ more and the ways of the world less. I have learned that I am perfectly imperfect and let's be clear, some days I am a straight up hot mess with yesterday's t-shirt, donning a messy bun with random glistening gray hair on display (where is that darn root touch up at again). Sweet friends, guess what? That is just fine with me. I am HIS mess. He knows I am flawed, and I know that I am flawed too. Sisters, we need to love on each other and encourage one another. We need to join forces as a strong tribe of women who are there for each other through the storms of life. Ladies, be prepared as there will be storms, but hopefully the storm of *perfectionism* is no longer one of those storms.

Over the last year, I have observed a great deal of posts on Facebook. I have acknowledged how people tend to manipulate real life to fit their version of their Pinterest worthy life. I'll be honest I have been guilty of doing just the same. You know what I am talking about. When pictures are staged to show only the best of life- the house tidied and decorated to the nines and the kids looking like tiny runway models. I believe this puts out a distorted view of reality vs. Fakebook. You saw that right, Fakebook. So many people live their lives for the next picture or post for social media, but only the ones where everything is shiny and flawless. Let's be real, like genuinely real. From my home to yours, here are some real-life happenings. Wednesdays are late start, meaning the kids start school at 9:00 a.m. instead of 8:00 a.m. I enjoy this extra time to do my Bible reading and devotionals, as well as getting a head start on knocking out some laundry and reviewing my calendar for work and review emails. I had noble plans of making a gourmet(ish) breakfast, getting the kids up early and spending some quality time with them. Well, the reality is, I apparently hit the alarm off button on my phone instead of snooze and woke up at 8:49 a.m. 8:49! One thing to note is we live approximately twenty minutes (**15.5** ACTUAL miles) from the boys' school. I tugged on my Christmas moose or is it reindeer slippers (girl, who actually cares, they were literally $0.75 at the Wal Marts) for shoes and screamed like a straight up crazy lady for the kids to get ready. This was without a doubt, not my finest parenting moment. Wait, let's add insult to injury, today is only Wednesday and I hate to admit it, but it is a repeat of Tuesday- alarm and all. Both Tuesday and Wednesday, we arrived at school in a cloud of smoke on two wheels. Yesterday and today were reflections of real life. I try to share both the good and the not so good on social media. I want to be real. Mamas, we are struggling together. We need to keep it real and encourage each other through those trying and just plain insane moments.

I am not here to bash on social media. It actually can be very useful when properly used. I think the point that needs to be driven home is *"when properly used."* I have recently unfollowed some of my Facebook friends because of their very misrepresented life on Facebook. I also have taken note of who I am truly friends with. I have no interest in helping someone reach a higher "friend count" on Facebook. Let's be real and not paint a twisted view of what

My Reality: My Messy Life

your life is actually like. Y'all, life is messy. Sometimes it is exceptionally messy. Take the picture, whether the glittery silver strands of hair are on full display and shining through or not. I think some of the best memories are made during the messy parts of life. I definitely do not want to indulge in the façade of living reality one way and putting something completely different on Facebook or other social media platforms. I want to ensure that my social media posts are truly reflective of who my family and I really are. I am perfectly, imperfect. I am flawed, but I am His and My God is actively pursuing me just as He is actively pursuing you. My life is messy, stressful, and chaotic but somewhere in all the crazy there are moments of pure bliss. You know those moments, when the kids are getting along, and they are doing it on their own I might add. It is the moments that you savor, and you just want more of. You are afraid to blink for fear that the moment will pass too soon. When your teenage daughter is so on fire for God that she finds her voice and she begins to write music and sing that music to praise the Lord. You know, when your sweet dog Chloe runs to see you after a long day, that first drink of a hot cup of coffee, or that super awesome dreamy moment as a family when you are all together and giggles fill the room or the impeccable sunset that you cannot look away from. I long for those moments during times of chaos. I share on social media the messy and the blissful aspects of my life. I know that the mess and chaotic are what other mamas are enduring too. We should not shy from who we really are. I challenge us all to walk in the real life vs. your picture-perfect social media presence. We are struggling together. And if you got it all together, then God bless you, you precious little thing please teach the rest of us how it is done because the majority of us are over here on the struggle bus day in and day out.

I could not help but think of this Bible verse in Ephesians 5:8 (ESV) "For at one time you were darkness, but now you are light in the Lord. Walk as children of light." That is so good and so true. It is darkness before a relationship with Christ, but once you have the intimate relationship with our Lord and Savior, you have the calling to be a part of something bigger than yourselves. You are the light in your homes, schools, and places of employment.

Chapter 2:

THE ENEMY

I almost skipped this chapter on the enemy. I did not want to write it, but you know what, the Bible talks to us about the enemy and we as believers, we need to prepare for battle. The enemy is a master manipulator. He will attack where you are weakest. He has a way of attempting to possess your thoughts. The mind is so easily infiltrated by the enemy. The enemy has vowed a spiritual warfare within our mind and often we are oblivious to said warfare, especially in the beginning. The enemy is evil, cunning and is willing to do whatever it takes to accomplish his task of total destruction. Oh, but wait, he's not done. Nope. Not even close. The enemy will drudge up her past and bring about those hurts to keep her completely off her game. He will take her to new lows and pledge to keep her there. It will take a holy intervention for her to start fighting back, let alone win the war. Sweet sister, it is time to put on the Armor of God and go to battle with your greatest foe. A verse that will stop the enemy dead in his tracks comes from Ephesians 2:4-10 (NIV) "But because of his great love for us, God, who is rich in mercy, made us alive with Christ even when we were dead in transgressions – it is by grace you have been saved. And God raised us up with Christ and seated us with him in the heavenly realms in Christ Jesus, in order that in the coming ages he might show the incomparable riches of his grace, expressed in his kindness to us in Christ Jesus. For it is by grace you have been saved, through faith- not by works, so that no one can boast. For we are God's handiwork, created in Christ Jesus to do works, which God prepared in advance for us to do." This verse is my battle cry. Sweet friends, this verse is now our fight song. This verse speaks life. God has never-ending love for you. Through the acceptance of Christ, we die to our sins and we a find new life with our Savior. So, let's get to work.

Struggling with the enemy began, well in the beginning. Eve was living her days in the Garden of Eden and along came a sneaky serpent. Eve was the first woman to have the enemy speak lies to her. In this moment, the course of history changed for all humankind. The serpent made Eve question God and the promise he made with both Adam and Eve. The enemy has always been crafty and methodic in his tactics. The enemy knows that this tactic works. Self-doubt is very dangerous especially when we allow it to be used against us.

The enemy knows our weaknesses and he knows

precisely when to strike and where to strike. He knows we are not immune to his wicked ways. His mission is to steal, kill, and destroy anything and everything in his path. He will use any means necessary. He will infiltrate our thoughts and deceive our truth. I have allowed the enemy to invade my thoughts and fill my thoughts with his lies. I have allowed him to place these and other strongholds in my life. I permitted him to have power over me. Y'all, I gave up my authority and permitted the enemy into my heart and mind, time and time again. It took me awhile, but finally I had enough! I hope that you reach this point as well. Sometimes it takes us strong-willed gals a little longer to come around and see the error of our ways. I was done being vulnerable and I finally reached a point where I was irrefutably done granting my joy to be robbed by the enemy. Within us is the greatest weapon to defeat the enemy. We have innate design to need an intimate relationship with God. A relationship that is fueled by our continual spiritual growth and pouring into our relationship with Christ. We can enable our weapons by getting into the Word of God regularly, thanking, praising, and worshipping the Lord. Simply put, GIRL READ YO' BIBLE! Know the Word of God, apply by living the Word of God on a daily basis. We need to start by taking the time to thank God for all He has done and not done in our lives. We need to dive into God's word and give our Bibles one heck of a workout. We need to worship and praise God through song or conversations. Psalms 7:17 (ESV) "I will give to the Lord the thanks due to his righteousness, and I will sing praise to the name of the Lord, the Most High."

I have struggled with being enough. Any guesses where my antagonist decided to attack? Oh yes, the enemy led an all-out assault (raid) on my self-worth. He led me down a path where I felt inadequate as a wife, mother, daughter, friend, and employee. It was a no holds barred air strike with vicious intent from the enemy. He wanted me to be down for the count. He wanted me to be in a state of self-loathing. Unfortunately, I was granting the enemy the ability to overtake me. I gave up fighting for myself. I *allowed* my joy to be seized. Well, thank the Lord this is not where my story ends. After an epic pity party, I simply said, "God, lead me and take control. I can't do this alone." I opened my Bible and dug in. I searched for scripture, I cried out to God and slowly started to fight back. I knew scripture, prayer and worship were three of my greatest weapons to defeat the enemy. I began to see my prayer life take off like never before. Girls, I was super simple with my prayer life. I sought verses that were simple but resilient. Philippians 4:6-7 (NIV) "Do not be anxious about anything, but in every situation, by prayer and petition, with thanksgiving, present your requests to God. And the peace of God, which transcends all understanding, will guard your hearts and mind in Christ Jesus." This verse was everywhere. I needed constant assurances from this verse in the beginning. It was my lock screen on my phone. As my faith matured, I could lean on this verse without the need to see it physically.

We need to push back on the enemy's callous advances. We need to find lay our burdens at the feet of the cross and let God. Wow, strong words, but one of the most difficult acts of faith for me personally. It is okay not be okay all the time. However, it is not ok to live down in the shallows. Girl, it is time to fill your ears with worship songs, your mind with scripture, and your heart with His promises for your life. A great verse that I lean on when I feel like I am in the middle of spiritual warfare is Psalms 139:14 (NIV) "I praise you because I am fearfully and wonderfully made; your works are wonderful; I know that full and well." I am created by the Creator. I have been created for His purpose.

The enemy has a way of attacking us where we are most vulnerable. Relationships, family, finances, and self-worth are just a few examples. Personally, I have been struggling with self-worth and the feeling that I am not enough. I have had doubts that I am not enough as a wife, mother, friend, employee, and now distance education specialist (aka home iPad education patrol- keeping them off YouTube since March 2020). I have had legitimate fears that I will fail my children, my husband, my family, my employer, my friends, and myself. The fear of not being enough has really come to life in these last few weeks. In the last couple of weeks, I have called out to God more times that I can count. I have prayed to the point of crying and eventually falling asleep more times than I can count. We are all in this together. We need to press into God through these challenges and lean on his Word. We need to take things one day at a time and allow for a whole heaping of grace. At our house, when I am struggling, I start talking to God out loud. I want my kids to know that this is how I handle my battles. I take them to the One who can handle them much better than I can, and I lay them at His feet. Each morning after spending time in scripture, worshipping and praying I am better equipped to handle my days. I am a better mom, wife, daughter, friend, and employee. Most days, I put on my headphones and crank up some worship music to power through the day. Current times are beyond what any of us have ever experienced. I had the lofty idea of setting this amazing schedule broken down to the forty-five minutes that my kids would play outside. Friends, I went to bed at 7 p.m. on day one.

Seriously, I needed to adjust my unrealistic expectations (here it is again) of what our days would look like. Day one was full of tears, jeers, and fears! The struggle was real. The students in my house were dancing awfully close to be expelled and the self-appointed Assistant to the Assistant Principal was about to get a boom box and blare some jams to commiserate the resigning of her self-appointed new position after twenty-three minutes on the job! After googling if boarding schools are still open and then realizing the price tag, we decided we need to *amend* our schedules and expectations. When we need a reset, we like to *dance it out* at our house, well the kids and I do. Keith, not so much. So, on day two, I woke up the kids, cranked up the volume on some KLOVE and we *danced it out.* One of our family's favorites is "Grace Got You" by MercyMe. Try to listen to that song and not move. IMPOSSIBLE! We usually follow it up with some NKOTB (for those of you who do not know New Kids on the Block.) #TeamDonnie. We danced, giggled, and smiled. Our hearts needed some fun in the midst of the chaos and unknown.

Stay on task with your walk with God. Continue to pour into this relationship. The enemy will be persistent in his attacks. The good news is, we know the ending.

Chapter 3:

Oh Goodness...I Am A Wife

I can remember dreaming about who I would marry as a young girl. As a teenager, I would practice writing what I hoped my married name would be. Like many of you, I am so grateful for unanswered prayers. I had the delusional idea of marrying someone like prince charming, move into an amazing home, and begin building our life together. Oh, my goodness, I almost forgot the bravado of living happily ever after like every Disney fairytale depicts. I think I just gagged a little thinking about marrying prince charming and the fairytale happily ever after. This is an unreal expectation. I had to learn that I was not a princess and my husband not a prince. We were just two people trying to figure out how to do life together. In the beginning, we tried to this this marriage thing without God. Big mistake. Little did I know merging two completely different lives can be challenging to say the least. I had some totally messed up ideal that everything would just magically fall into place. We would be so happy to be married that nothing would get in the way of that happiness. Uh, wrong. Marriage is not easy. It is hard. A good marriage takes effort from both parties. You have to continually invest in your spouse and your relationship.

While we are hitting all the tough topics, let's just hit the one that almost everyone has an opinion on…submission. This word has an innate ability to make people uncomfortable. I will be the first to admit that this is an area that I have struggled with in the past. I am extremely self-sufficient. By nature, my personality is quite the opposite of someone in favor of submission. I can be a bit on the bossy side and I certainly like things to go my way. I am more of an extrovert and my husband more of an introvert. Y'all submission is tough for us bossy gals. I will be completely honest, it is tough. Like **real** tough. It is through my faith walk that I decided to be open minded and gather information and knowledge with regards to biblical submission. Here is what I learned, submission to God is a necessary step in the Christian walk. Jesus's suffering on the cross at Calvary while knowing He had to be submissive to God to fulfill prophecy, even though it meant terrible suffering and death. Jesus would submit to the Father and experience horrific punishment. It is through that most selfless act of Jesus, that I want to work harder on relinquishing my own agenda and living my life in biblical submission to God.

When Paul writes in Ephesians 5:24 (ESV), "Husbands, love your wives, as Christ loved the church and gave himself up for her..." I want my husband to put Christ first. I work to put my relationship with Jesus as the focal point in my marriage. I feel that this allows me to honor my husband and our marriage. When our kids were smaller, I put the kids before my husband. I do realize in doing so I neglected my relationship with my husband. At one point in time, we had three children under three to say we were busy with raising kids would be an understatement. It was challenging to make time for each other. As our kids got older, we were able to make more time for each other. It was not easy but we both knew our marriage was more than worth it and marriage takes effort by both parties. I am here to say that if Jesus would have been at the forefront of my marriage when my kids were younger it would have made a huge difference in how we communicated with each other and how we parented our children. I tried to handle everything on my own and that was not a very wise idea on my behalf. I regret struggling with my faith and not having a personal relationship with God during this time. I wanted faith when it was convenient for me. Here is the thing though, Jesus never stopped pursuing me. He never stopped chasing at me even when I would resist and turn away. How amazing is our God that He meets us right where we are?

In the past, I have stretched myself so thin that I would literally stress myself out. During the COVID-19 outbreak, I have focused on self-care and priorities for myself and for my family. My heart needs peace and contentment. My family needs peace and contentment. Before COVID, we struggled to find time together to enjoy the simple but important things like eating dinner together around the kitchen table. Our family life needed a "demo day." It was time to get back to the basics of being a family devoted to living for Jesus. We have enjoyed our time together. We have thoroughly deep cleaned our house, put up Fort Knox type fencing to keep our little mini petting zoo safe and have started the process of building Kinsley a new "beach themed" room in the garage. The enemy loves to attack matters of the heart. Your schedule, your time and your energy are all fair game to his deceptive plans. We have kept our promises to never fall back into the complete chaos that was our family unit before covid. We make sure that we have time together as a family to eat dinner, watch a movie on PureFlix or have a karaoke night. This is an area that I am not willing to concede when it comes to my family.

The opposite of busyness is idleness. There is something to be said about being stagnant. Sometimes you just have to put on your big girl pants and get the job done. A Proverbs 31 woman does wait for things to happen, she makes them happen. There is a distinct difference between rest and idleness. Rest is a time to pause and reset, a refresh if you will. Idleness is a state of stagnant nothingness.

One of my favorite verses throughout the Bible is Proverbs 31 the Epilogue: A Wife of Noble Character- hence the title of this book. This verse speaks to me in a very real way. Details of this verse. This wife will do her husband good, and not evil all the days of her life. She is strong, hardworking, and more than capable for her tasks. She is so worthy. This passage can really hinder one's thinking and think that is this unobtainable for any woman to live up to, but it's not. These characteristics are a guideline for King Lemuel from his mother in finding a suitable wife. I have started praying this verse over my sons when I am praying for their future spouses. I pray this over my daughter as I hope that she knows that she is worthy of a man that will treat her as if she is more valuable than rubies. I pray that all three of my children find spouses that are desperately chasing Jesus.

Remember early on when I said I debated buying a cast iron skillet for a little marriage demo? Well, here's a little story of that wife who is a terrible cook. When I was younger, my mom made baked chicken and rice. Oh, how I loved this meal! It was one of my favorites. I decided as a newly married woman that I should make this for my husband. That was a terrible idea. Absolutely horrific. The rice was crunchy. Side note: rice should not be crunchy. I do not think that Keith has ate much rice since that awful meal. I think I almost killed us with the salmonella too. Chicken might have been slightly under cooked. Okay, it was still pink. I have come a long way in my cooking abilities. I am no longer terrible but don't ask my family how often we eat angel hair pasta and marinara.

I am a big fan of romance. I love flowers. I remember when Keith and I first started dating, this guy hit the area of romance out of the park. He wooed and I was smitten. One look from this man could make me feel like I was the only person in a crowded room. Here we are after eighteen years of marriage. Our marriage has changed and evolved. We have made it a priority to put God first in our marriage. It took me a long time to get to the point where I was putting God first. I wanted Keith to be this perfect man who could meet all my needs. I placed him on a pedestal where he could never achieve at the level, I expected from him. I put Keith where I needed my Savior to be. I was failing my husband left and right. In the past, I may have acted like a bit of a princess. Marriage is tough. Marriage is self-less. It took me a long time to learn how to love my husband well and to not be so much of a princess. It also took me time to learn how to fight well. I struggled with disagreements…I don't know, something about always needing to be right and struggling with forgiveness. As you can see, I was not allowing Jesus to be the center of this marriage. Keith and I began attending church together at Living Proof. (Love my LP Family!!) Our lives changed in so many ways. We had other couples pouring into us and praying for us. These church friends have become our sweet family. I also had to learn that our marriage was evolving just as Keith and I were changing. We made it this far by the grace of God and lots of sweet prayers. Our children have so many people pouring into them and loving them through life. My daughter has a tribe of the most amazing young men and women at our church that she is doing life with. I think it is such a blessing for these young adults to take time out of their lives and speak life into her and her friends. Sometimes, I just catch myself smiling and loving how far my family has come in our walk with Jesus. There is no mistaking that God is moving in this rural Kansas church. I am humbled to be a part of something so amazing. How good is our God!

Chapter 4:

My Family

My family. They are fun and crazy. They are wild and passionate. We do not always agree. We have some hot tempers. We argue about some of the dumbest things, probably due to the fact that we are passionate folks with hot tempers.

My parents raised a daughter who is extremely independent and perhaps a little quick to voice her differing opinion. One of my favorite moments, is watching my parents as grandparents. God created my parents to be grandparents. They have grandkids who adore them and cannot wait to be with them. As like any other relationship, we will fail each other but at the end of the day, we are each other's most devoted supporters. I want nothing more than to be surrounded by my parents and siblings at church. Keith prays each and every day that our families will be at church with us.

One the of the most amazing moments in my life was witnessing my sister let her wall down and give her life to Christ. You want to talk about a situation that will cause you to experience all the feels at once, well, this situation would be one that would fit the bill. I have since witnessed my sister grow in her faith and lean on Jesus during the tough times and in the moments of triumph. We have always been close even though there are nine years between us. Sometimes, it has been more of a mother/daughter type relationship. She is quick to remind me when I get a little too motherly. This woman is and always will be one of my very best friends. I am amazed at the woman, wife, and mother she is. She fought and scraped her way through nursing school while taking care of her young daughter and being a wife to Kyle. My sister and I share a very similar path to motherhood. It was not an easy path. Never in a million years, did I ever think that I would be thanking God for letting me endure what I did to become a mother, but I am truly grateful for my experience so I could be a true source of support when my sister went through the same situation. Our past hurts have forever created a bond and have allowed us to support each other in the healing process.

My brother is one of the most passionate people I have ever met. He is an amazing dad. He loves his kids fiercely. I wish that we had a better relationship. We are both pretty head strong people, passionate and both very much like to be right and get the last word in. I pray for our relationship to grow. I hope that he knows that I will always have his best interests at heart and perhaps, I could step back on trying to mother him since he is an adult in his thirties. Randall, I will be saving you a seat at church, as well.

My grandparents…man they are some good people. They are the type to do anything for anyone. They give the best advice. They love without hesitation. They are just genuinely good people. I am beyond blessed to be able to do life with them. They have always loved me, not necessarily always agreed with my gypsy soul ways but they have loved without ceasing. My grandma is my role model for a prayer warrior. She has a running prayer list by her bedside table. I now try to write down all my prayers. My grandpa Leon, this man has influenced my life in more ways that I can count. These two have enriched and blessed my life beyond measure. I know my grandma's prayers will not get me into heaven, but I am certainly thankful that she continues them.

My husband, Keith is one of the greatest blessings in my life. I am grateful that God gave me this man to do life with as husband and wife. He truly gets me. He knows that I have this hard to tame wild side and a temper to boot. He also knows that I am someone who values time with loved ones and takes an hour to say goodbye. In my defense, I am observing the true Midwest fashion of goodbyes. Yes, it does take approximately an hour to say goodbye. You would think that I am in some black and white movie preparing to go off to war or something. I am saying goodbye and my family lives roughly thirty minutes from me. Thank you, Lord for this man and his patience. I know being my spouse is not easy.

My kids. Man, I love these kids. I am grateful that God allowed Keith and I to parent these sweet kids. I have always wanted to be a mom. Becoming a mom was a struggle for me. I struggled with infertility issues. I never knew this struggle would be a life issue that would forever bond my sister, Tiffany and me. Let me tell you something, God was faithful even when I was not. He knew the desires of my heart. He made me a mom. I always tell my kids that they were created from scratch. Well, that has changed to God created them from scratch. I love being their mom. Do not get me wrong, not every day is a walk in the park. Some days, I am in the trenches with these kids. I make a point to apologize when I am wrong, and I apologize often, more than I am proud of and more than I like. I want them to know that I do not have all the answers, but our God does. And to find those answers, we need to seek God. I am doing this parenting thing wrong probably more than I am doing it right, but I have a God that gives grace like confetti, and I spend most days, standing there with arms wide open.

McKinsley (Kinsley) is our sweet teenager with a heart of gold. This girl has a deep love for Jesus, and she will do amazing things. She has a passion to help kiddos with special needs. She loves softball. This girl is a patriotic, American who loves her country, the flag and what it stands for. She is just a joy to love on. She just wrote her first song after attending #despo21.

Brody is the oldest of the twins. He is quick to remind everyone he comes in contact with that he is older. He definitely has the older brother persona. Brody is an old soul. My sweet twelve-year-old loves John Wayne, old Westerns, anything Army related, and old hair band music. He is basically like a fifty-year-old trapped in a twelve-year-old body. He has a soft and gentle heart but is fiercely protective of his loved ones. We call him the sheepdog as he protects the sheep.

Brogan is the baby of our family. Brogan has a strong will and a zest for life. This kid has confidence in his corner. Sometimes we have to dial down the confidence. Brogan is extremely loving and sincere. He loves Louis Armstrong and Michael Bublé. Brogan and Kinsley enjoy singing karaoke on evenings we are all at home together. Ah, the sweet belly laughs that come with those evenings.

The LP Youth kids are just like my own. I love these

kiddos. We are also doing life together through youth group and friendships with my kids. I am honored to be able to give back to the kiddos in our community. These kids are on fire for God. This generation, they were born for this time. They will be our future pastors, worship leaders, evangelists, and missionaries. Guess what? With this amazing group of worshippers at the helm, the future looks pretty darn good.

You know it takes a village to raise a family. I am blessed to be a part of a tribe that has this amazing opportunity to do life together. I am grateful that our friend's kids have become like ours. We have been able to enjoy vacations together, celebration high school graduations, weddings and our friend's daughter going off to college. We have made wonderful memories; we have prayed for these kids. Our village is a blessing beyond words.

My church family are some of the most faithful and encouraging folks. I am beyond blessed to have friends who have become family. The family we have gained through church have blessed our lives in ways I cannot begin to describe. We get to stand along-side each other as a village and love each other well. Thank you and we love you all! Canasta anyone?

My sweet, heaven born babies. I have wanted nothing

more than to touch your sweet little cheeks as you slept in my arms. I have longed to watch you roll over and take your first steps. To dream about your future. To watch you take your place in this world. I have been envious that I did not get the opportunity to hold you, gaze at you, and smile uncontrollably as new mamas do. I wanted to watch you grow up with Kinsley, Brody, and Brogan. I would have given anything to keep you here, but Jesus knew that you were too beautiful for this life on Earth. It took me a long while to be grateful that Jesus took you to be born in heaven. A piece of my heart is already in heaven. I will always love you to heaven and back. Xoxo

Chapter 5:

MY HURTS

On April 21, 2003, my heart was in shambles. I was broken. I felt defective and worthless. I did not even begin to know how to mourn the loss of a baby. This situation was a pivotal event in my life. First, it was the beginning of a very dark place for me. I remember walking into a cold procedure room. I remember the sweet nurse that met Keith and I in this room. I will never forget her clutching my hand and crying with me and whispering sympathetic and encouraging words. Forever burned in my memories is the sadness in Keith's eyes. I could not shake the feeling of thinking this not how this is supposed to go. This is not part of my plan. I was angry, hurt, and shattered. My heart ached for this baby. From the moment of two pink lines, I could not wait to see Keith as a dad. I knew he was going to be amazing. I was ready to see him in action, but reality told me that would not be happening yet. I spent several days in the hospital as I struggled with heavy bleeding and dangerously low blood pressure. I felt like I was outside looking in at myself. And what I saw was a frail and broken young woman full of such heartbreaking sorrow. During my hospital stay, I had to be wheeled into the hallway due to a tornado touching ground nearby. I really did not want to go in that hallway. I did not want to engage in conversation. I did not want to see anyone nor have anyone see me and my brokenness. I had a deep fear that someone was going to ask me what I was in for. I just knew they could see right through me. They could see a young girl who was defective and broken. I glanced up as a sweet older gentleman caught my eye and…he… simply…. smiled. A smile so sweet and so perfectly timed. I did a double take because I was sure that it was my grandpa Joe who had passed away almost a year before. I knew in my heart this was no coincidence. That sweet smile was all it took to break down my walls and open the gates. I tried to fight back the tears; I did not want to cry but I could not fight it anymore. I was wheeled back into my room got into bed and cried until I fell asleep. After being released from the hospital, the cycle of anger, hurt and depression would rear their ugly heads. I would walk away from a job I enjoyed because of overheard comments and corresponding hurts. I should have been an excited young woman planning a wedding to an amazing man. I was not excited at all. I loved Keith there was no doubt about that. I was in such a state of shock and unimaginable pain that I could not shake it. The pain was so deep, and I wanted nothing more than to bury those hurts, put them in a box and not deal with it.

My heart began to close off to the outside world. I spent the next several months shifting between anger and extreme guilt with a whole lot of uncontrollable tears. I confided in my Grandma JoAnn during this time. We would cry together because that is what we did. If one was crying, inevitably the other would join in. My heart ached. Her heart ached for me. I do not remember us saying much other than just crying but those moments were precious and what my heart needed to start healing. I needed God so desperately during this time of my life. I was beyond resistant to let God in. In my mind, he let this happen. He allowed a sweet, innocent baby to not experience a life outside the womb. I was so angry at God. I completely and without a doubt, wanted nothing to do with a God that could take away a baby from its mom and dad. I needed a scapegoat and I used God every chance I got. Looking back, oh my, how I needed God. My heart needed the love and reassurances from God. I know that God never forgot me and continued to love me. He never gave up on me. We would experience a miscarriage several months after the ectopic pregnancy in April 2003. During this time, I received a book that referenced 2 Corinthians 1:3 "Praise be to the God and Father of our Lord Jesus Christ, the Father of compassion and the God of all comfort, who comforts us in all our trouble with the comfort we ourselves receive from God." As much as

I wanted to continue to blame God, I knew I was wrong. I was honestly numb by this point. My desire to rock my own baby was met with adversity and its fair share of heartache and challenges. In February 2004, we again saw those two pink lines. I tried to distance myself from this pregnancy. I let fear intercede and control me. I remember going in for the ultrasound. I remember trying to beg with God that everything would be okay. That would not be the case. The ultrasound tech was extremely quiet. She was having trouble locating a heartbeat. I remember the look we exchanged, and the tears started to flood my eyes. I knew, I just knew. I could not and would not look in Keith's direction. I failed again. My doctor came in and we tried to find the heartbeat again. Nothing. My heart was once again torn to shreds. This pregnancy ended in a miscarriage. I was beyond broken. I felt like such a failure. For Pete's sake, I am a woman, and our bodies are designed to carry a pregnancy and I was defective. I seriously felt like I was less of a woman. I was a mess and broken. I apologized to Keith. I had so many horrible thoughts running through my mind. Why would this guy stick around? I mean he wants kids, and I am BROKEN and DEFECTIVE. The enemy continued to hit me when I was already weak and struggling. He played tricks with my mind. I can remember again confiding to my grandma JoAnn. I needed God so desperately and

I was fighting and resisting Him with everything I had in me.

I began to seek fertility help. Then my grandma got sick. She was diagnosed with lung cancer in April of 2004. The Lord called my sweet grandma, JoAnn home in July 2004. I postponed fertility treatments. Roughly a month after my grandma passed away, I found out I was pregnant again. This is when my heart softened towards God. God blessed not Keith and I but my entire family with this amazing little baby. This baby was sent from heaven. On April 15, 2005, we welcomed with loving arms McKinsley JoAnn Beattie. I used to tell Kinsley, "Be careful, remember I made you from scratch." Well, that thought has evolved as it should to, "Kinsley, remember, God has made you from scratch."

On Kinsley's third birthday, Keith and I learned we were expecting again. We were not surprised to learn that we were expecting as I had to see a reproductive endocrinologist. I began to think something was a bit weird when I would go in for lab work to see that in a forty-eight-hour window my levels were tripling. So, at six weeks along, Keith and I went to the endocrinologist office for our first peak at our newest little addition. As a woman who has saw an empty womb on a screen after learning of a miscarriage, I held my breath till we would hear a heartbeat or see a life on that screen. The ultrasound showed a sweet little pea with a strong heartbeat. And I could breathe again. The nurse and the doctor looked at each other and smiled. Weird, but ok. Dr. Stewart moved behind Keith and then came, "There are two heartbeats." Keith looked like he saw a ghost. I cried because well, that's what I do. On November 26, 2008, our family grew from the starting three to the fabulous five. Brody William and Brogan Matthew arrived on one of my favorite holidays and two days before our first baby's due date of November 28.

One thing that I now hold near and dear is that whether I am in a peak or valley, a storm or during the calm, I will praise God. It is not easy, but nothing worthwhile is particularly easy. It has been a journey to learn what it truly means to press into God during my valleys and storms and stay consistent while in times of peaks and the calm. God is omnipresent. He will never leave us. He is always there ready to engage us in conversation, prayer, and worship.

We can reflect on Job's story in the Bible. Job is a man of great faith. God allows Satan to interject challenges into Job's life. After losing his children, his livestock, servants, and wealth; Job then fell to the ground in worship and said, "Naked I came from my mother's womb, and naked I will depart. The Lord gave and the Lord has taken away; may the name of the Lord be praised." Wow! Talk about a strong foundation. Job was a man of unwavering faith. I regret not having the stamina and strength of faith that Job possessed.

Chapter 6

From Broken to Blessed

I have been in a place of despair, just like you. I know what broken looks like. I know what brokenness feels like. Take a look at the world around us. Brokenness in every direction. Whether we are mourning the loss of loved one taken too soon, the loneliness of lack of communication with others or the sheer volume of a broken world with anger and hostility running amuck. Our hearts are hurting.

I was damaged goods. There was once a time that I thought I was so damaged that I was beyond repair. I did not understand how God could possibly love me. I could not even wrap my head around what that kind of love really meant. I would love to be able to tell you that this was addressed in my youth but that is not my story. Like you, my heart has ached. There was a time that my heart was aching to be a mom. After several losses, I wondered if motherhood would happen for me. I would wonder down the baby aisles at Target and Wal-Mart. I would always find myself at some point in tears. I am sure anyone who saw me was thinking what is wrong with her. And then I saw her. She was doing the same thing I was doing. Our eyes met and we knew without speaking a word we were facing the same fight. You see, after an early pregnancy loss such as an ectopic pregnancy and miscarriage there is no burial. There is no real goodbye. I guess this was my way to cope and say goodbye and to mourn our babies and maybe even find hope. During this time, I knew who God was. However, I wanted nothing but distance between me and God. I was angry. I felt like a failure. But mostly, I was hurting. I needed God but instead of turning to him, I blamed Him for the reason my heart was in shambles. The enemy found a way to entrap me, and I allowed it when I turned away from God.

You see, the enemy attempts to frustrate and alienate believers from God. The enemy tries to create a wedge that cannot be overcome. I think the enemy uses the power of the mind to wreak havoc on believers. We see that Job stood firm in his authentic love of God and passed the tests of faith orchestrated by the enemy. Satan's attempting to defraud believers at every available opportunity. If you have not read *"The Screwtape Letters"* by C.S. Lewis, I highly encourage you to do so. This book provides so much insight as to the method and manipulation utilized by the enemy.

I read two amazing books by Angie Smith that began the healing process for me. *I Will Carry You the Sacred*

Dance of Grief and Joy and *Audrey Bunny* Sidenote: Angie Smith's heart story through these books helped me begin to heal. I am grateful to Angie for her sharing her life so I could find a way out of the pit and on to the healing process. And I began writing my own book. I talk in more detail about my journey, and it has been so good for me. Writing has always been my outlet. And last but, certainly not least, I made amends with God. I laid years of anger, resentment and hurt at His feet. And with that, my heart softened, and the healing truly began for me because I know that those babies are resting in the arms of our heavenly Father.

You see, we all have a back story that is the subject matter to our individual testimonies. I know there is another woman who is going through or has gone through a similar situation as me. I want to support her through her brokenness and be an encourager. I do not recommend the route that I took. Remember running from God is not a good idea in any circumstance. We should be running to the Father. I needed God and I would even go as far to say that I knew that I needed Him, yet I refused to let Him in my heart. Yet, He continued to pursue me. He did not stop. I pushed and pushed, and He never gave up on me. That my friends, is what God's unfailing love looks like in real life. It is just that simple. The love of God is unlike any other kind of love you ever experience. As humans, we will fail our loved ones, not necessarily on purpose but we are humans and that makes us fallible. You guys, He approached the woman at the well. The woman with multiple husbands and who was outcasted by her village. He did not care whether or not she "looked or acted" like the atypical Christian. He could care less about appearances. He is all about seeking that personal relationship with **YOU**. A moment in the presence of Jesus and that woman high tailed it into the village to share her story of her encounter with the Messiah.

Thomas struggled with doubt, yet Jesus included him in his inner circle. Jesus left the ninety-nine to find that one lost sheep. The one with a back story who is going through something and needs a moment in the presence of Jesus. Maybe that sheep is you. Maybe you have been running and you are tired. I get it. Heck, I was you. It took me awhile being hard-headed and all to realize that Jesus wanted me just the way I am in that moment…a mess who was struggling with hurt, unforgiveness, anger and what I believed to be a jaded past. What I mean by jaded past is that I believed in my heart that He did not want to save me and for some reason I was too far gone for God to step in. I could not have been more wrong. He was not waiting for me to get it all together and He will not be waiting for you to get it all together either. He wants to take our brokenness and begin mending us right exactly where we are at. He wants our weakness, our brokenness and our past and He wants to make you new. His desire is for you to lay your burdens at the foot of the cross and begin a new life in relationship with Him. This is just one of the amazing parts of our testimony, aka the backstory.

From my experience, suffering introduces humility. As humans, we are not profoundly fond of humility. Humility can make us appear vulnerable. I am not one to love the state of vulnerability. Humility tends to showcase our imperfections. However, humility opens the door and allows God's grace to break down walls. 1 Peter 5:5-6 (NKJV), states, "yes, all of you be submissive to one another, and be clothed with humility, for God resists the proud, but gives grace to the humble." Our God calls for us to humble ourselves before Him so we can begin a more faith filled journey with Jesus at the helm.

Suffering is deeply personal. This is where we need to personally lean on Jesus. Psalms 34:18-19 (NIV), tells us "The Lord is close to brokenhearted and saves those who are crushed in spirit. The righteous may have many troubles; but the Lord delivers him from them all." In Psalms 147:3 (NIV), "He heals then broken-hearted and binds up their wounds." You guys, simply put we are asked to humble ourselves before the Lord and allow his sweet grace to break down the walls. You can never be so broken that God does not want a relationship with you. You are the very one that He will leave the majority of his flock to pursue. There is no such thing as so far gone that Jesus does not want a relationship with you. In fact, throughout scripture, we see that Jesus seeks those who are known to be cast outs, He evens seeks the criminal who is being crucified with Him. It is time to stop making excuses and time to find it in your heart to humbly seek a personal relationship with Jesus.

It took me a long time to wrap my head around the fact that you do not have to "look" a certain way to be a Christian or have #Christian'cred. There is no "Christian look" per se. In fact, a Christian comes in all walks of life. Being a follower of Christ simply means that you have the heart of a servant and accept Jesus as your Lord and Savior and invest in nurturing that relationship. You can wear the shirts and say the things; but it does not hold true if you are not walking the walk. I recently shocked my close family and friends, well some of my close friends were in on this. We were at a Women's conference in Branson, Missouri. Somehow, tattoos came up. Well, we found a place and they could get all five of us in to get these tattoos before our next session later that evening. I got the words "YOU ARE enough" on my wrist. Stay with me here. I got this particular tattoo for a couple of reasons. I wanted to honor God during my praise in worship in that YOU ARE (God) enough. When my hands are raised, I am proclaiming that Jesus is all I need and through Him, I am enough. It is a daily reminder that through Him, I am enough. I cannot do it alone, but through the grace of God, I can do all things. I love that I get to share this hilarious experience with some of the best gal pals that a girl could ask for whether they got the tattoos or provided moral support.

It is no secret, that I like to review scripture for my blog, but I also try to find a song that drives the message home. The song "Truth Be Told" by Matthew West has been the song that I have listened to and reflected on while writing this book. None of us have it all together. None. He does not call us to be perfectly put together. No one is perfect except, Jesus. God is seeking those that are broken, those who are hurting, those that are struggling. The Bible is full of His peoples' stories who are broken and struggling. I know I have said these several times by now this is bears repeating, Jesus meets them right where they are at. Rahab was a prostitute. I would say that alone would signal that her life was less than ideal. Rahab was actually named within the Bible. That alone has significance. She also was instrumental in helping the Israelites capture Jericho. God chose a young, Jewish girl in Nazareth with strong faith to be the virgin mother of Jesus. This my friends, is where the amazing grace of Jesus comes in. He wants our brokenness. He wants us to lay our burdens at his feet. God met Rahab and Mary exactly where they were, women of little significance and then God changed their lives and used them as vessels for His glory. And my friends, it is a given fact that we will have burdens and suffering. The Bible tells us in John 16:33 (NIV), that there will be suffering. But in this pain and suffering, there is so much potential for growth and sweet, sweet grace. And then God gives us a great promise when he says, "But take heart! I have overcome the world." God's grace for his people is one of the most amazing gifts he reveals to us. We lean on Romans 8:28 (NIV) "And we know that in all things God works for the good of people who love Him, who have been called according to His purpose." I look at it like this, you have a choice to make: (1) you can continue to run from God and try to handle life and adversity on your own or (2) you can run to God in the midst of your storm and allow God to take the wheel. I would encourage you to choose the second option. I tried the first option for far too long and it never worked out for me in the long run.

Our family recently watched *God's Not Dead 2* and there was a phrase in the movie that shook me to my core... Walter Wesley said: "Honey, you of all people should realize when you're going through something really hard, the teacher is always quiet during the test." How many times have we complained that the Father is quiet even after fervent prayer? I was close picking myself up off the floor because that statement shook me to my core in that moment. The quote is so simply but this is exactly the issue I have been seeking answers to for several months. I have been working on this blog for a while now. And there it is just as plain as day…*the teacher is always quiet during the test.* We must trust his timing is always good. I have struggled with it being His timing and not mine. The test or the storm is the time to really press in and seek God. Read scripture, praise the Lord, worship all while giving Thanks to the creator of Heaven and Earth for He is good especially in the storm and the timing will always be on His authority.

I do not have it all together. Some days, I do not have anything together. I could very well be in the same t-shirt I wore the day before, hair not brushed, looking like a hot mess. But at the end of the day, I am HIS, mess and all. I want to give God all the glory for He is good all the time. Our God is so amazing that He loves us exactly where we are. Romans 5:8 has been paraphrased to say, "I loved you at your darkest." The Creator of Heaven and Earth is loving us through our times of trials and tribulations and when we are dead in our sins and transgressions. Jesus is and always will be there every step of the way. It is so hard for me to exactly comprehend that kind of love. But I think simply put it means YOU ARE NEVER TO FAR GONE FROM THE LOVE OF THE FATHER. Let me say it again for the girl in the back row…your God loves you unconditionally sweet friend. He loves you in the valleys and on the top of the mount. I am grateful and humbled by the grace of God and His never-ending love.

My past is just that, it's my past. My past does not define who I am, nor does it define you. I saw a Facebook meme that said something along the lines of… my past is like an old address, stop trying to reach me at the old address because I no longer live there. We are made new through the blood of Jesus. How amazing is that? So, girls let's not sit and dwell at our old address, let's enjoy our new life at our new address with Jesus at the helm.

Chapter 7:

A Forgiving Heart

I am a blunt person by nature. I am guilty of speaking before thinking. Words typically expel out my mouth and then it becomes clean up aisle nine. I am also guilty of thinking of a catchy come back phrase rather than listening to what is being said. In this situation, I pray for more Jesus and whole lot less Tara. Sometimes a little too late, hence the clean up on aisle nine.

Brutal honesty here, forgiveness has been one of my greatest struggles. I am way too quick to respond and extremely slow to forgive. I have been known to have a sharp tongue. I have been guilty of thinking I should be quickly forgiven while taking forever to forgive others. I have a hard time letting go of past hurts. I take things to heart. One thing that has helped me is to pray for those that have hurt me or that I think have hurt me. I cannot count the times it was a simple miscommunication that caused unnecessary issues. When I purposefully pray for a person whom I am struggling to forgive, I notice it takes the sting away and it frees you to let go of the lingering hurt. It helps me get my perspective right on the situation. I am guilty of expecting grace instantly but taking my sweet time with giving grace. I know this is an area of strife for me. I have to put effort into working through forgiveness. Forgiveness is described as the *decision* to release feelings of resentment or vengeance toward a person or group who has harmed you. Also, notice the word "release." YOU have to choose to let go and move on. Yes, girl, *YOU* have to put in effort when forgiving. I know, not easy. Even as a believer, it is not easy for me to forgive. I think sometimes I can get caught up in how this or that hurt made me feel. There are times when I misconstrued what the other person was actually saying. I am far from perfect over here. I have really tried removing my hurt feelings from the equation. I notice I tend to dwell on how I am feeling about the situation rather than offering forgiveness. I am in a constant struggle with forgiveness. I notice when I really try to remove "the emotional attachment" I have to the situation it helps me be more forgiving.

Forgiveness is hard. It requires a person to surrender. Forgiveness is not easy or fun. Forgiveness requires an action on your part. Forgiveness, often times requires humility on the person doing the forgiving. Forgiveness has been a labor of love if you will for me. I have committed myself to exercises to find ways to forgive others to move on and seek peace from whatever that situation may be. I have relied heavily on scripture to make progress with forgiveness.

I have leaned on Psalm 130 as I want to serve the Lord with a joyful heart. Past hurts and bitterness have been keeping me from serving in the manner I should. Psalms 130 (NIV) states, "But with you there is forgiveness, so that we can, with reverence, serve you. In Luke 1:77 (NIV), "...to give his knowledge of salvation through forgiveness of sins." I cannot grow in my walk with God if I do not allow forgiveness in my heart. As noted in Acts 26:18 (NIV), "to open their eyes and turn them from darkness to light, and from the power of Satan to God, so that they may receive forgiveness of sins, and a place, among those who are sanctified by faith in me." When you are in a state of bitterness you cannot move forward or thrive in your faith, you are stuck in a logjam position in your spiritual walk. In Matthew 6:14-15 (NIV), "For if you forgive other people when they sin against you, your heavenly Father will also forgive you. But if you do not forgive others their sins, your Father will not forgive your sins."

Along with struggling with forgiveness came deep seeded anger. I let the enemy set up shop and steal my joy and in place of that joy he left anger, resentment, and irritability. I was not the mom, wife, and friend I wanted to be. I was stuck in a rut and for the life of me I could not find my way out. I stayed in this deep, dark hole much longer than I should have. I questioned how my family made me feel like I was their personal maid. I would be cleaning the house while my family sat around the house on phones, iPad and watching TV. I would glare at them as if it would accomplish something. I would begin slamming cabinets and scoffing to show my disapproval of their lack of assistance. Nothing. They did not even recognize my passive aggressive dance that was on full display. I would go to bed angry and wake up angry. Someone always left a cup lying around or used a paper towel and left it on the island rather than walking four steps to put it in the dang trash can. These people were driving me insane. Actually, it was the enemy hard at work fueling the fire that was raging inside of my mind. The enemy was testing me, and he was winning yet another war against me. Without realizing it at the time, I was in the midst of spiritual warfare for my mind, and I was losing. I had a very sweet lady tell me to pray for family members as you do household tasks such as tidying the house and washing and folding the laundry. I thought *you have got to be kidding me*. Was my husband actually paying attention to my passive aggressive house cleaning and asked this lady to have a little chat with me? I double hate doing laundry and why would I pray as I folded laundry. Weird. I mean I despise doing laundry. This seems like a husband's secret trick to get his wife to do the laundry- maybe? Regardless, I thought *okay, could it really hurt to try this approach to tackling the laundry?* So, I dove in and tested this new method of doing laundry. While I folded my husband and kids clothing, I spent a lot of time in prayer. Jesus and I had a humbling but sweet moment right then and there. In the clean laundry basket was an old preemie onesie of the boys. I thought *okay, I see what you are doing here God*. In that moment, I realized how fast the years are flying by and how Jesus is always faithful. Yes, he was faithful even while I was a runaway Christian. At that moment, I got why that sweet woman did some of her best praying while doing the laundry. On a side note, there are supposed to only be five people living in this house, the laundry made it seem more like ten plus lived here. All joking aside, this is one of the greatest things I have started doing when it comes time for household chores. I love this quiet time to pray and reflect on my family. It is quiet time that you can devote to praying for your husband and children. These days, I am proud to say that some of my best work for Jesus is done while doing the laundry and cleaning the house.

Chapter 8:

THE QUIRKY SIDE OF THINGS

I feel distracted when the house is untidy. The chaos of untidiness makes me feel out of sorts. I get antsy and easily annoyed. Okay, let's just be honest here, I actually straight up lose my mind when things are out place, so my mind is pretty much gone on most days. When everything is smelling good, tidy, and organized I am at peace. I have at times wondered if I have house cleaning ADD. I run around cleaning one room and then get distracted and move on to another room because I see something else that needs my attention in there. A wise person would focus on the bathroom and knock it out and then move on to the next room. I have tried that method, but the distraction of seeing something else that needs done, will entice me to a new locale. I am in such a frenzy to get everything cleaned that I simply create more work in the long run. I have three children who are more than capable of helping as they should. I will again share some honesty; I will redo the work they do. Not because they do not do a good job but because I am obsessive with how I want things done. I should be thrilled with the help. This is another area in life that I am working to having realistic expectations while not missing out on the good times with my family.

I am also the mom that has a well thought out plan ready for action if a rogue lion escapes its enclosure at the zoo and then channels in on its predatorial instincts and begins hunting the people at the zoo. My husband just looks at me and shakes his head. I just think it is part of my risk management personality that thinks we need to be prepared for such events. Being a mom pushes you to a whole new level of yourself or more accurately a new level of crazy. I have had moments of pure bliss being a mom. I have heard through the grapevine that I can be a bit of a helicopter mom. I am the one who puts the kibosh on my kids cooking dinner without supervision because I have the most insane thoughts running through my head that my kids are going to touch raw chicken, lick their fingers and then cause an outbreak of salmonella or listeria. They are 16, 12 and 12, and I know they are smart kids and are not going to handle raw chicken and then lick their fingers or something, but I think it is worthwhile to heed on the side of caution. Instead, I remove any possibility of that scenario playing out. These kids are more than capable of cooking dinner, and they are not going to touch raw chicken and then lick their fingers. I mean who thinks this way? Me. I think this way. Motherhood has completely wrecked my brain and caused me to have some very irrational fears.

I have a hard time relaxing. Like a real hard time. I am thirty minutes into a sixty-minute massage and the massage therapist is still telling me to relax. I can't relax because while I should be relaxing, I am going through **"mama to do the list**." You know **the list**, the ever-growing, never-ending list that all mothers have in their head at all times, especially times when you should be focusing on something else. You cannot remember that you ran out of milk while walking down that aisle at the grocery store but at 2:34 a.m. you wake up because you remember you need pop tarts and not just strawberry because not everyone likes strawberry, so you have to get cookies and cream too. Oh, but wait, you get this crazy but pretty brilliant idea that maybe you should make homemade pop tarts in your free time with the kids as a fun activity to do together. Sometimes the list shows up while you are in mid conversation with someone. That's always fun.

When Kinsley was in preschool, I had to talk myself out of calling the school. I had in my mind that I needed to call them and inform them that she was a wanderer and to keep a close eye on her during recess. There was a definite possibility that she may try to dart from the playground. Especially, if she sees a stray cat or dog, she gone. And no one will be the wiser. Perhaps, I should remind them to count all the kids before returning into the school before recess.

What about the stragglers? My kid is a straggler or maybe dreamer is more accurate. She has been one to stop and see and experience the beauty in the world around her. Anyone else ever done this? No? Just me? Great! I mean this kid's favorite trick was to hide in the clothes racks at stores and watch me freak out and go into a panic and then she would start giggling uncontrollably. I should have known.

I am that mom who worries if my mom will remember to keep my kids from playing in the street at her house. It is so nothing against my mom. I love my mom and know that she is more than capable of looking after my kids, but I have irrational thoughts because being a mom is tough and it literally makes you crazy.

As you can tell, I am not a risk taker. I never have been. I am far from it. I despise roller coasters; the Ferris wheel literally makes me sick to my stomach and bubble wrap is a necessity. My lack of taking risks does not mean I am not fun. I am plenty of fun. Unfortunately, I have noticed that I have a bad habit of projecting my fears onto my kids. I want them to experience the wonderful opportunities that life offers and live life to its fullest. I also want them to be safe while doing so. I am the mom that put the snorkel mask up to my face and started flipping out and had to abandon my kids and husband as they snorkeled in the

Caribbean Sea while on vacation in Montego Bay, Jamaica, and Isla Mujeres, Mexico. Fear crept in kept me from joining them in making some wonderful memories. Also maybe sharks and fear of the water in general. I am a mess I tell ya. There is a picture of Brody underwater snorkeling with two thumbs up. It is a picture that he loves because he loved this adventure. I am glad that my irrational fear did not stop him from an experience he loved.

I am pretty quick off the cuff and sometimes I pay for my words. I love Jesus and I need a filter. Most days I need a filter. I do not mean to offend folks… well, most of the time, I do not mean to offend anyone. I just speak and do not think. My words can be awkward. I mean I once asked someone if they intentionally chose to name their kid what they named him. I asked a friend when she was due, and she had the baby months before- not once but twice. I cocked my head to the side and made some weird noise like wahh. Totally awkward. I typically apologize A LOT.

I like to believe that God has a sense of humor. I am sure I keep Him more than occupied with my crazy antics. I imagine He responds with a smile and a head shake.

Chapter 9:

CAUSE MOMMIN' AIN'T EASY

Let me be real here. Motherhood is anything but sunshine and rainbows. Some days are exhausting to say the least. Do not get me wrong, there are so many beautiful moments of motherhood. There are times where I need a moment, so I do not have "a moment." A moment to myself where I can have a crazy, pity party, meltdown of epic proportions. During these moments, I am calling on a holy intervention as these sweet angels have just tested their boundaries yet again. I remind our kids that your father is gonna agree with me so good luck with that nonsense you are doing as I walk by with a tub of lemon cookies heading towards my closet. Pity party/ meltdown ensues and then comes the phone call to my husband. Oh, I am sure he loves the panic stricken, psycho wife calls. I am willing to bet that he thinks I have lost my ever-loving mind. After Keith's motivational speech I am sure similar to Coach Dale's on *Hoosiers*, I feel empowered to take on the world. Sort of a *I am Woman Hear Me Role* persona erupts within me. I have got this. I have got this. They are kids and I am the adult. What I do know for certain is that once I start praying out loud when my kids are acting like fools, they know it is time to scatter as fast as humanly possible.

There are these perfectly put together moms who look like they just walked off a runway and then there is me who is looking like a hobbit in over-sized sweats and my college t-shirt that is so old it has holes from excessive wear. For some moms, it just seems like they have it all together. The hair, the kids, the husband, the house, heck, even the pets. Well, not here. Nope. Not. At. All. I am some version of a beautiful disaster. I forget things all the time. I stand people up all the time. Not on purpose. I cannot help but to think I am a terrible mom. I am failing my kids. I am failing God. Kids are demanding. They push us to our limit; limits we did not even know that we had. But in the middle of this sticky, messy life there is a moment of beautiful surrender. Sweet friends, I LIVE for these moments.

I need to change and find contentment in the mess. I am where God has purposefully placed me. I try to do it all by myself without leaning on God who is so **BIG.** He is so much bigger than any of my issues or failures. Through Him and with Him I am more than enough. I have a habit of getting caught in my personal failures. I had this insane thought that motherhood would be perfect and blissful. I expected the most well-behaved children. I always wanted to be a mom. I wanted the dreamy husband, check, well most days. I am my own worst critic. I am hard on myself. Raising children is tough and definitely not for the faint of heart. Some days you are in the trenches, and you are just praying for reinforcements. I am not going to lie, there are days where I hide in my closet and eat an entire box of cosmic brownies loaded in high fructose corn syrup and I do not even care. You do what you need to survive. I am parenting two kids who are people pleasers, and one is a very strong strong-willed young man. A strong-willed parent who is parenting a strong-willed child is like a head oncollision of personalities. I know this young man will do amazing things in life. We just have to make it to adulthood with him.

I wonder am I supposed to feel happy every day? I mean genuinely happy. Am I doing this mom thing right? Am I failing? Am I failing my kids? Am I failing the bar that I set for myself? Am I failing God who entrusted these kids to me? How do I know if I am doing any of this right? Being a mom has made me feel more vulnerable than ever before. I thrived as a mom when my kids were little. My entire world was wrapped around these sweet kids. The older they got, the more I struggled with thoughts of not being enough and thoughts that I was failing them. As any mom, I want the very best for my kids. I want them to do great things in life. I want them to find success and happiness. But above all, I want them to know to put God first and others second and self third. I want them to be humble and kind. I want to see my adult kids in church worshipping with their families. I hope when my time is done that they know that I loved them more than they will ever know.

I have been guilty of comparing myself as a wife and mom to other women. I have looked on Facebook and thought to myself, *Wow, she has got it together or she has to have a nanny or some sort of help.* We are bombarded with stuff from every direction. It is constant through tv, Facebook ads, the world is constantly testing our mind with the whole comparison guilt trip. We are constantly being told how to look and what to do to look a certain way. We are shown how our homes should look, how we should over-schedule our lives with activities. It is all around us and certainly from every single direction possible. I am guilty of falling victim to this comparison game. I remember thinking that my kids need to play a musical instrument, so they have an artistic outlet. Play sports for physical activity and the skills to learn to work together as a team. They needed to learn a foreign language, so they are cultured. Uh, no. My kids are well adjusted and love God. They are far from perfect, but, hey, we all are.

Some days, I raise my voice more than I would like to.

Some days, I am stretched thin and my husband, my kids and even my work do not get the best of me. I have been using our time at home to really focus on being the best me I can be for those who are dependent on me. I am taking care of my mental health and physical health by walking lots of miles to take the time to reset, meditate and have my walks with Jesus.

I love being a mom. I always wanted to be a mom to a large family. I have always loved kids. Being a mom is beautifully amazing. It is messy, chaotic, and beautiful at the same time. When I am having one of my moments as a mom, when I feel like I am not enough. I grab my headphones and press the play button. I listen until my heart find peace because I know that God is surrounding me with his endless love and his sweet, sweet GRACE. I would say a great deal of my struggles as a mom are self-imposed. I get caught up with high ideals of how certain scenarios **should** play out. I do not give myself enough grace. I focus more on what I could have done rather than focusing on what was accomplished.

We also need to lean on each other as women and mothers. We should not be in competition. We should be the one's speaking life and encouraging each other.

Chapter 10:

Here Comes the Boom: Stress Overload

It starts with one thing that is usually quite minor. Then that one thing turns into two. I quickly start to feel on edge. I am still reeling from the first incident and then it is several rows of dominoes have been knocked down. Everything starts to slowly and methodically begin to unravel. By this point I am reaching stage five crazy woman status and there is not much that can be done to de-escalate the situation. I can promise you that I am not reacting in the best manner to the situation. I would love to say I do but that would not be accurate. I have started calling out to God when this begins to happen. It is helpful for me to calm down. I am sure I look insane to someone from the outside watching this go down because my hands are up, and I am in the middle of spiritual warfare. Let me just put it this way, a strong-willed mama and a strong-willed child are going to do battle from time to time. It is inevitably going to happen.

I make the time to spend time with God each morning. I usually have a little Thanksgiving chat with God before even getting out of my bed. I make sure to spend time reading and studying the scriptures. I spend time throughout the day listening to worship music. I set aside time to pray and continue my morning chat with God.

What stresses you out? How do you handle that stress? What can you do differently to better handle the stressors in your life?

When it comes to anxiety related stress I want to lean on God. I want to give God all my burdens. All. Of. Them. Girls, this is not easy. Nope, not at all. I am a self-professed control freak. There is not a situation that I do not like to control. I have resisted giving my burdens to God. Plus, when you add the fact that I have a domineering "care-taker gene," you see how a control freak may slightly lose their mind, right? After years of "trying to do it all on my own," I decided it would be a good idea to give God a little test to see how He handled my burdens, you know before I completely let Him have them. Um, ya, not something I would advise anyone to do. Y'all, God is in the business of handling burdens. When we really rest in His Word, we see so many times the Lord has fulfilled His promises. In Proverbs 14:1 (NIV), "The wise woman builds her house, but with her own hands the foolish one tears hers down." What we can learn from this verse is so simple but so profound. Build a strong foundation by pressing into God's Word and stand firm on God's promises. Press in.

Whether you are a working mom outside the home or inside the home…you are working. I am currently a working mom both inside and outside the home. The current drive to my office is a little over an hour one way, of course depending on the mess of traffic that particular day. As a part of my job, I travel to our office in Buffalo, New York to spend time working from that office. I enjoy traveling to Buffalo. It is a beautiful city, and the food options are the best. Sounds amazing right? Here's the low down, I have been in this same position roughly three and a half years. I read, review, and redline legal contracts for SaaS related products that my company specializes in. I also am a mom of three kids. And I was exhausted, over indulged, and depleted. My daughter, who is sixteen, enjoys high school basketball and competitive softball pretty much year-round. We are in the beginning phases of exploring colleges. She is in high school, so we have tons of games and other activities to spectate. And the twins. They are involved in travel baseball and play basketball. Three kids, tons of activities. and two parents. The odds are stacked against us. Oh, and I forgot to add that my husband is an industrial electrician for a construction company who is busiest during, that's right spring and summer ball season. I was always running late to events and activities. Something had to give, I was running on fumes. I decided I needed to switch things up. My boss and I chatted about increasing my ability to work from home as a possibility. My job has allowed me the flexibility of telecommuting. There is added stress with working entirely remote as well as trying to ensure that my kids were getting everything done with online distance learning. There are days where I have said go outside and play, we will try school tomorrow. My kids were like caged animals. It is more than challenging to get them to sit down and focus on their schoolwork. I am not going to lie, sometimes, I bribe them. Some days I yell and some days I just consider the day a wash. I am an adult woman, and this is hard on me. I am conflicted about what "role" I need to be during various times of the day. There is no real division in the day. I filter back and forth between mom, employee, and wife. In between Zoom meetings I am trying to keep caught up on the laundry, making sure everyone is fed and schoolwork is completed and sent in. What a novel idea that you need to send homework in. One minute I am reviewing and redlining a contract and the next I am trying to understand my kids' math. New math, what is new math, um, well, it is a nightmare. We are a carry the one family.

My job is demanding. It challenges me on an intellectual level, and I love it. I love to grow relationships with our customers and to sometimes have to have some pretty intense conversations as we negotiate a contract. This job has taught me how to stand up for myself. How to be bold in what I want and no longer fearing a "no" response. I have noticed my workdays that begin in the word and through prayer for the day that lies ahead are more successful.

Chapter 11:

I AM HIS: HOW TO BE A PERFECTLY IMPERFECT PROVERBS 31 WOMAN (HOT MESS)

Prayer

My prayer journals are not fancy, in fact, they are simple, wide-ruled spiral bound notebooks. These notebooks are filled with prayers, pleas, joys. You can see tears were shed over these pages. My prayer life has become more intentional and purposeful when I committed to writing down my daily conversations with God. I hope that one day my children can reflect back on these journals and see how their mom fought her battles, with God by her side.

I can pour my heart out to Christ through my prayer journal. I can feel my relationship grow with Christ through prayer. I usually start by just saying how good God is and how I am truly thankful for all answered and unanswered prayers. Yes, those prayers we used to say when we were younger and who we wanted to marry, those qualify. A big thank you for those unanswered prayers, am I right? I love to play worship music or some sort of relaxation music while I am praying. My prayer journal is covered with random thoughts and prayers. Frankly, it has no rhyme or reasoning behind it. Some pages look like a letter to God, others are covered in my favorite worship songs, and some have random Bible verses and names. I like to mix it up I guess you could say. If I am out and about and do not have my journal with me. I will add notes in my phone or take a picture of a Facebook message with my phone and then transfer it to my Journal. It is neat to look back at the progress and growth of my prayer life. In other words, if I am say praying for you, you better believe you are capturing some space within the lines of my journal or in the notepad of my phone. I love this simple way of keeping myself accountable. I love to write meaningful things down. It is simply what works for me. I am sure there are wonderful apps in which you can expand your prayer life. I think that main thing is to find an avenue that fits best for your life.

God is so good. He loves us in the peaks and in the valleys. He wants a personal relationship with us. A great way to cultivate that personal relationship with God is through prayer. You can find some amazing books, blogs, and other resources on prayer, but to me prayer simply means having a conversation with your Savior. My prayer life started pretty simply. "Jesus, I need you." My prayers have evolved but not by much. It is simply a conversation with Jesus and that I need less of me and more of Him in all areas of my life.

Chapter 12:

Worship

I grew up attending the Catholic church. I loved my little hometown church. I loved the people that made up this church. I loved our priest. He was not your typical Catholic priest. He was an older gentleman who wore leather pants and rode a Harley. He had a zest for life and deep love for Christ. Attending Catholic Mass in my small hometown was what I knew.

As someone who grew up Catholic, I never understood how people worshipped with their hands raised and danced in the aisles. I am guilty of calling these folks the "front row Hallelujah sisters." I could not help but wonder, when are the snakes going to make their appearance and what is wrong with these strange people. The raising of hands was so completely foreign to me. I grew up attending services that were extremely regimented. I loved the structure of it all. I knew what to expect and I found comfort in that.

My life began to take a turn that I did not see coming when we started attending our current church, Living Proof, close to where my family lives. I know I have said it before, but I love our church. It is a church family based on a relationship with Christ not a membership to the church. The church is the family, and the family makes the church. I felt a calling to re-dedicate my life to Christ. Moment of truth, I debated rededicating my life to Christ for nearly a year before I finally gave in. I even tried to psych myself out of following through with the re-dedication that day of. In all honesty, I felt myself growing closer and closer to God, but the enemy got in my head again. Little did I know, my life was about to be forever changed. So, in my thirties, I got baptized. This time I did it for me and because I wanted to live my life for Jesus, for the rest of my life.

I am not a singer. I honestly cannot carry a tune and I feel so sorry for those who sit near me at church. I am not sure my noise is joyful, but it is done with a joyful heart. In the past, I would mouth the words but did not really vest my time into worship. I knew that I could not sing and was worried if others heard that horrid noise how they might react. So, I tolerated the singing to get to the message, you know the real reason you come to church- or so I thought. I will be extremely vulnerable and honest and say that I had a stirring to raise my hands long before I ever did. I knew God was telling me to re-dedicate my life to him through baptism but raising my hands… nope not happening- I decided to dig my heals in and fight God on this one. I full-heartedly believe that it was the Holy Spirit trying to grab ahold of me and I resisted. I wanted a relationship with God, but I wanted this relationship to be on my terms. I was embarrassed to be considered a Hallelujah sister, I thought these gals would have raised their hands and shout hallelujah at about anything. Honestly, I kept thinking about the Mississippi Squirrel Revival and let me tell you, a squirrel running crazy in church was the ONLY way this girl would be raising her hands at church.

A few years later (yes years, I am a little head strong), I went to Desperation, a youth conference with Kinsley in 2018. I went with the purpose of getting Kinsley from Kansas to Colorado to Wichita for a softball tournament. I was not expecting this to be a life changing event. I was not planning on experiencing one of those spiritual "ah ha moments." Nope, I was planning on fading into the background until it was time to go. While at Desperation, I was surrounded by thousands of teenagers who were on fire for God. One of those teenagers was Kinsley. It was almost like I was on the outside looking in, again. I never really witnessed her worshipping. I was humbled and blown away. Kinsley is one of those kids that is on fire for God. This girl worships like it is just her and God alone in a room. She is all in. I remember just being overwhelmed with emotion watching her. This was another moment in which I started crying and could not stop it. Deep down I knew the blockage to a more meaningful and deep relationship with God had just been busted wide open. My hands went up and my heart opened to God like never before. We recently got back from #despo21. My heart needed this event. I am telling you, there is no more humbling experience than when you are in an auditorium with thousands of kids who are actively and fearlessly worshipping the Lord with all they have.

Throughout the Bible, we hear of characters "worshipping." Psalm 95:6 (NIV) says, "Come, let us bow down in worship, let us kneel before the LORD our Maker." Worship and prayer go hand in hand. Psalm 29:2 (NIV) shares, "A scribe to the LORD the glory due his name; **worship** the LORD in the splendor of his holiness."

I wish I would have had a better relationship with God when Keith and I experienced early pregnancy losses, when my grandma JoAnn passed away, when our twins were born and needed to stay in the NICU and when Brody broke his femur. In each of these moments, I needed that relationship with God. I needed those assurances that only came from an intimate relationship with God. I needed that peace that comes with having a strong foundation in Christ. Instead, I had what I would call religion and wavering faith and sometimes, sadly I had very little faith. I carried the weight of the world on shoulders that could not endure that type of burden. Even when I was not engaged with Christ how I should have been...HE was still there. He brought our family the sweet blessing of Kinsley when our hearts mourned the loss my grandma. He knew we needed a gentle soul to mend our broken hearts. Sometimes, I am blown away by their similarities- like crying on cue and having this amazing heart filled with love for kids at St. Jude's. God was also with us in the NICU. He loved on us when we were treading on new paths. He was most certainly there with us when Brody broke his femur. He comforted our son when he should have been in horrific pain. He calmed our heart as we raced to the emergency room to get Brody the care he needed. When I was not present with the Father.... He has *ALWAYS* been PRESENT for me.

    I do not always sit on the front row, but yes, I am a hallelujah sister! I still cannot carry a tune and the kindest way to describe my singing is a *joyful noise.* Heavy emphasis on noise. Sweet friends, let me tell you, raising my hands and truly worshipping God has transformed me and my faith walk. I have a deeper personal relationship with Christ that entails worshipping, praying, consistently reading the Word of God, and daily conversations with God. I start my day with worship music. I clean the house to worship music. I love to go outside during the Summer and worship God amongst the stars and the fireflies. I fight my best spiritual battles with biblical scriptures, worship music and prayer. I will praise the name of Jesus through the storms. I will praise and raise the name of Jesus at the enemy and unbelief. I believe in the hope that comes with being a believer who is in pursuit of a relationship with Jesus. I don't think that means all my prayers will be answered in the manner I want them answered nor will they all be answered. It means that I am coming to God with my concerns, and I rely on Him and Him alone. He can handle my burdens. I am simply not equipped as a fallible human being to handle such things. I am able to find peace knowing that I stand firm in God's presence and the plans He has for me.

I have caught myself losing sight of how BIG God really is. I have tried time and time again to lean on my own understanding or perhaps more truthfully how I feel. I am so small compared to how truly big God is.

I liken myself to a wild horse. At times, I can be flighty and quick to take off and then there are times where I need that social interaction during my timing- of course. Then there are the times where it seems like I am galloping with my head in the clouds…just dreaming of running completely wild and free. But not the wild and free you are probably thinking of. My wild and free has transformed over the years to something quite amazing. When I think running wild and free, I think of heaven, my real Home. I think of being wild and free with my heavenly Father. I see an eternity with no pain, no worries, no anxiety, no drama- just complete amazement in with the presence of Christ and that I just am trying to take it all in.

I love that my sweet friend Angela has encouraged me in "walking with Jesus." See what we did there? We enjoy Facebook Live'n while we are walking with Jesus. You guys! This is a great concept at heart. Walking with Jesus when you have a super long driveway in the middle of nowhere is nothing short of a great idea. I pop in the air pods (for the longest time I was certain they were called ear pods) and crank up some praise and worship music and belt out to Chris Tomlin and others. I also enjoy podcasts such as "DareToBe." I also use this time to pray. This has been wonderful to spend time with Jesus each morning. I enjoy listening to the Bible in the morning while walking as well. This time helps to get my mind right before starting my work or time with the family on the weekends. This time is a devotion to be with Jesus.

I am growing in faith every day. I have the most amazing tribe of church gal pals that hold me accountable and love on me and provide encouragement to me as a mother, wife, and woman. These women also love on my kids in a big way. These women help me pursue my relationship with God. They have stood in gap in prayer for me. There is something incredibly powerful about having some of the most amazing prayer warriors by your side in life.

It took the COVID pandemic for me to realize the true importance of observing a day of rest. I want my Sundays to be devoted to a day of rest in the arms of my King. I have really been focusing on taking the time to listen to worship songs, write out my prayer requests, reading and studying my Bible and simply laying my burdens from the busy week at his feet and just resting in his presence.

This is more important now than ever. It is critical for moms to find some sort of normalcy during the current pandemic. But more importantly, it is necessary for moms to take care of themselves so they can give their best to the other members of their family. These days self-care looks a little different. We may squeeze in a bath at 10:30 at night when everyone has finally gone to bed. An amazing spa experience may look a little something like a Vitamin C Epsom salt bath that is uninterrupted paired with a two-year-old face mask to "cleanse" my pores, followed by me plucking "glittery looking" hair from atop my head while donning a charcoal face mask. Speaking of hats, I recently texted a friend and said I think I need you to talk me out of a good idea. Boxed hair dye. Response was, please don't. Girls- if I have one piece of advice it is to avoid dying your own hair. Many instances will turn out okay. However, some of us, me included, have no idea what I am doing, and it will cost more to correct it because I will end of with some weird variation of fire engine red while attempting to cover the gray that is shining through my normally brown hair.

Sometimes you make a detour to the nearest Petland to spend time ogling over sweet puppies. I love puppies. I especially love puppies that I do not have to clean up after. Well, that is not a true reflection of who I am. I just love puppies and dogs. My kids look at me in disbelief as I tell all the puppies that I love them. Perhaps, it is a little weird for some, but it is my truth. I have not met many puppies or dogs that I do not love.

Self-care is opening your Bible and getting into your Word. Self-care is participating in Bible studies. It can be holding yourself accountable with other women as your press into your relationship with God. I am grateful that 2020, and all the nuances that came with 2020, have allowed so much growth in this area of my life. It is critical to take advantage of the time we have to really nurture our relationship with Jesus. I am learning something new each time I open the Word of God.

Let's be real, some days, I am standing outside yelling at Satan to go back to hell and to leave my family and loved ones alone with tears streaming and worship music blaring. Nope, not all days are five-star experiences, sometimes self-care looks like eating junk food like twinkies or zingers in my closet, alone.

Chapter 13:

SWEET JOY

Joy. I know, I know. Why does she need to write a chapter about joy? I debated writing this chapter. After careful reflection and prayer, I decided this chapter was more than needed, it is necessary. I needed to write this chapter for myself. I mean I will be the first to admit that I do not radiate sweet, joyful vibes every minute of every day. Actually, quite the opposite some days. Some days, I have to fight to find my joy. I can let one cross word, or one more dang paper towel left on an island send me to a point of rage, you know, cast iron skillet type of rage. Seriously, I wish every day was filled with joy, laughter, and happiness, but it is not. Don't get me wrong, I am a joyful person. I love to be happy. I love experiencing life. I am on a mission to find the joy in everyday life. But joy, true joy, is a choice. I can choose to wallow around in a pit despair and anger, or I can choose to be joyful. This is a real challenge. I am working to retrain my brain that everyone is not a jerk wanting to wreck my world. Not an easy task, friends. I am working towards joy in doing the laundry- i.e. I am blessed to have a family to pray for while folding their shorts for the second time this week and oh hey, have I mentioned it is Tuesday.

Joy a state of mind and most importantly a choice. On my quest for joy, I quit the comparison game. I have been guilty of comparing myself as a wife and mom to other women. I have looked on Facebook and thought to myself, *wow, she does not scream that she is president of the hot mess express mom's club.* I believe as women, we should be building each other up. We should spend our time encouraging each other to keep fighting and persevering. The comparison game is just bad news. God wants us to be His feet on the ground. It is hard to reach others when you are stuck on the sidelines because you cannot get past the fact that Betty Lou has everything you want and don't have. You fall down the hole of then fighting the battle of feeling like you are not enough. Goodness, we create a lot of the issues we get into. Let me be really blunt with you sweet girl, the comparison game is a thief of joy. The comparison game has no place in God's plan for us. Galatians 1:10 (ESV) shares, "For am I now seeking the approval of man, or of God? Or am I trying to please man? If I were still trying to please man, I would not be a servant of Christ." We need to be willing to faithfully serve God right where we are.

We have a bit of a multi-animal hobby farm going on. We have one goat named Big Jake. What can I say, my twelve year old is more like a seventy five year old who loves John Wayne. We have a paint horse named Angel. I never believed my grandparents when they would tell little Tara- there are two ways you are sure to get hurt- horses and motorcycles. I learned that their wisdom on horses is true when the horse tripped, and Kinsley came down on the saddle horn cracking her bottom rib. Motorcycles, uh yep, I will pass on that one and so will my kids. No Keith, just no. We have two Dobermans Jordy and Daphne. Jordy is Keith's dog. Daphne clings to Brogan. Next is a Great Pyrenes named Chloe. Chloe is one of my greatest loves. She is two years old. She has the best personality. When I first got her as a pup, I wanted to name her Manhattan. I had some fanatic idea (see Chapter on quirks for further context) that she hated that name and that is the reason she did not come when I called her. It surely was not that she hard-headed and just did not listen. My Chloe girl has some interesting mannerisms. She loves food. She loves food so much that she will get right up in your face and love all over you and then let out a very un-lady like loud burp. Yes, my sweet princess burps like a man after devouring a huge helping of Taco Bell. She also has the gator roll perfected. Putting a leash on this girl is like taming wild horses mixed with trying to give a bunch of cats a bath. With all her quirks, she is incredibly sweet. This dog loves me. She loves to take her large paws and will gently paw at me with them. My sweet Chloe girl brings me joy. I love this dog. She is the perfect farm dog for this hot mess. Oh, chickens! You guys! We have chickens. First, I love farm fresh eggs. Second, I hate ticks and bugs and the chickens like to eat said gross bugs. Third, have you ever seen a chicken run? Oh man, that is about the funniest thing I have ever seen. I giggle watching them run across the yard. However, these are not your average chickens, they are like dogs and will follow me whenever I go. I like to think that they think of me as their mama, but let's be honest, they look at me and think she gives us the food. Here's the deal, I love animals. I love taking care of animals. Animals bring me joy. I am currently working on talking my husband into miniature donkeys and an alpaca or maybe two.

There is not much better in this world that sitting outside in the evening and watching the fireflies dance across the starlit sky while listening to the bullfrogs. I am well aware that I sound like a country bumpkin and that is just fine with me. For far too long I tried to pull away from my roots and who I am at heart. I truly love the simple things in life. Fireflies. Sweet tea. Hammocks.

I love nothing more than a good latte. I am a faithful patron of our local coffee shop, Café Latte at the Jackson. This little coffee shop is a popular meeting place for bible studies and gal pal get togethers. I recently took Kinsley and her friend Rylee to Golden Scoop in Overland Park. Oh. My. Goodness. This place is heaven sent. It is an ice cream and coffee shop that is employed mainly by folks with special needs. The joy in this building is infectious! Kinsley and Rylee both have hearts for those with special needs. We cannot wait to head back. This place is a God send for sure.

Sometimes, a victory is so small that you wonder if it can even be deemed a victory. I am here to tell you yes. A victory is a victory, whether large or small. You guys, I am declaring that ordering my groceries online, pulling into my designated spot and having some incredibly kind person load them into my car is a HUGE victory. Shout out to Paola Price Chopper! They have clenched a place in my heart!

When I finally reached the point of no longer seeking the approval of others there was such sweet freedom. This sweet freedom came after investing into a personal and meaningful relationship with Jesus. I do not let my past define who I am as a human. I do not let who others want me to be or who others think I am or should be define me. I am defined by who I am in Christ. I know that all the time God is good, and He is always for me.

I cannot write this book without speaking about my love for Branson, Missouri. Shoutout to Branson! Branson brings me joy. Branson is my version of the happiest place on Earth. This is clearly a city in the Bible belt for a reason. My family loves to vacation in and around Branson. We enjoy the outlet malls, the Landing and the Titanic Museum to see who can hold their hand in the cold water the longest or who makes it to the end.

One thing I learned throughout the COVID journey is that when we get down to it, we have very simple needs. Our wants have not completely diminished but our priorities in life have drastically changed and have changed for the better in my opinion.

Chapter 14:

HER VIEW ON THE WORLD

This world is not my home. As, you can gather from earlier chapters, I have tried to fit in with the ways of this world my whole life. I tried to keep up with the Joneses. I tried to be this Pinterest Perfect mom. I have tried too hard and too long to be something and someone that I am not. I failed. I was set up for failure from the very beginning. It took me forty years to figure out that this world is not my home. Message to the wise, please do not take forty years. Get it together long before I did. Like you, I am simply passing through this world. We are meant for so much more than the confines and corruption of the world around us. This world has the ability to tear you down in millisecond. This world looks to divide us. This world looks to attack our minds with corruption at every turn. This world does not equal a loving relationship with its Creator.

"My brothers and sisters, set yourselves apart from this corrupt generation. Be saints. You were not made to fit in. You were born to stand out. And in the words of Ronald Reagan, "Evil is powerless if the good are unafraid." These words are from Jim Cavaziel. This statement has been a life statement for me as I walk daily with Jesus. Every part of the above statement has such a prominent impact on my life. I do not want to be a part of this corrupt generation or world. I seek the truth and wisdom of God through scripture. I strive to be a walking, talking testimony for Jesus. I want those around me and those I am able to come in contact with to accept Jesus into their hearts and to have a personal relationship with Jesus. We were never made to fit in to this world. We were made for perfect relationship with God. It is really so simple that this world is not our home. Heaven is our home. We need to continue to do the good work that God has called us to do. We need to love as Jesus loves. We need to forgive as Jesus forgave. We need to be the feet of Our Lord while we are here on Earth. I am yearning for the day I meet God face to face to hear him say, "Well done good and faithful servant, your work here is done. Welcome Home."

1 John 2:15-17 (NIV) Do not love the world or anything in the world. If anyone loves the world, love for the Father is not in them. For everything in the world-the lust of the flesh, the lust of the eyes, and the pride of life-comes not from the Father but from the world. The world and its desires pass away, but whoever does the will of God lives forever.

John 3:16-17 (NIV) For God so loved the world that he gave his one and only Son, that whoever believes in him shall not perish but have eternal life. For God did not send his Son into the world to condemn the world, but to save the world through him.

I know that Thanksgiving looks a little different for all of us this year. The year of 2020 was one for the books for sure, BUT God has been so, so good and faithful. Yes, we are watching our world in turmoil around us but with a God perspective that view is a little different. Let's go deeper on this subject.

This year has thrown a great deal of adversity and chaos our way, including the diagnosis of new health issues, online education of our kids, working from home exclusively, stores running out of Clorox wipes, and no one will be able to forget the great toilet paper shortage of 2020. Living life during a pandemic has been something. But let's get down to the amazing things that we can take away from 2020 and 2021 to a degree. My family went on a much-needed pause in the Springtime of 2020. We were able to sit down to dinner and simply talk. No one had to dart out the door to practice. The sad but true fact was that we maybe had dinner together once or twice a week prior to the pandemic. I am beyond grateful for the pause that allowed my family to be a family unit together. Some of our best discussions as a family happen around the dinner table. It was the most amazing opportunity to just be in the moment together. I am grateful that I will take a stand I will value the family unit as a whole. We will not go back to what dinner looked like pre-2020. We have a new standard.

I am thankful for modern technology. I am so grateful for the ability to zoom, Facetime, and video chat. I find myself struggling with the need for human interaction. That is saying a lot because I can sometimes need time to decompress. I believe there is something to be said when something you normally take for granted is taken away. Modern technology has allowed our family to visit with family and friends. I have so enjoyed our Facetimes with my grandparents and parents. Of course, I would prefer to HUG them in a big way. If anyone finds a deal of hazmat suit, I am in the market.

I am also thankful to be able to explore adventures in cooking together as a family. The kids and I took advantage of Hello Fresh meals and were able to make gourmet meals together. This opportunity allowed Brogan to find a love for cooking that I dare to say, he probably would not have otherwise found. We also purchased a pellet smoker that has completely wrecked our dining world for the better. Um, all

I can say is get yourself one and your stomach will certainly thank you for it. You also might want to get yo' self some stretchy pants. I am grateful for the ability to see personalities show through when we cooked together. Kinsley naturally as a the first born, led. Brody liked the technical aspects of cooking but not necessarily the cooking itself. Our resident other forty-year-old, Brody, who lives in a world that is very black and white (he does not understand his twin Brogan who is 100% living in the gray) made us follow the directions line by line on the recipe cards. The conversation was nothing short of priceless.

Another big one for me is simply TIME, no, not the magazine. For example, my commute in the office was approximately an hour plus depending on traffic one way. Nowadays, I roll out of bed, read my devotional and Bible, and find one of the greats to tune in to. You know, like Louie Giglio, Jack Hibbs, and some guy named Bo Gerken. I have found myself turning to the Word, worship music and speakers of the Word more and more. I have found myself reading my Bible and researching online classes to grow my knowledge base. This is a good problem to have. I am without a doubt grateful for the TIME to be able to focus and dig deeper. I have been able to focus on writing for my blog and book. There is so much peace that comes from expelling my thoughts into written word. Peace and contentment are attributes that I have been able to find a lot easier these days. I am finding who I am through my relationship with Jesus. There is so much FREEDOM to be had with growing your relationship with Christ.

I turned the big 4-0 in November of 2020. I was seriously struggling with this number. I also randomly struggled with twenty-six- not entirely sure why. I am a bit quirky, I guess. After turning forty, I have realized that I am proud of who I am, imperfections and all. I cannot really say that about my 20's or 30's. I was constantly searching. I was searching so desperately for a relationship with the King of Kings. I did not know this then of course. I like who I am. I like who I have become. I am a perfectly imperfect mix of somewhere between an ample splash of hot mess meets a Jesus lovin' Proverbs 31 gal, who fervently loves her family and friends and tells every dog in her path that she loves them- type of gal. I am ok with that. I have no desire to be normal. Normal is what the world wants us to be. I am done with wanting normal. I have reached a point in my life where I am living for Jesus not the world. I am flawed and I fail but I am not quitting, I AM PRESSING IN DEEPER. You guys, I went from a woman who was a broken mess to a messenger. Well, I mean I am still a mess but through the grace of Jesus I have become a messenger. Join me! Let's grab a latte and have a little chitty chat about my Jesus and how he changed my life and can change yours too!

Prayers:

Jesus, I am thankful for sweet friendships. Thank you for blessing our children with sweet and encouraging friendships. May you continue to guide and nurture these relationships and encourage these kids and young adults to seek you first Jesus.

I am grateful for church services and the ability to worship freely. At the end of the day, we all know how the story ends. I will be transparent in the fact that there have been times where I have struggled with hopeless and anxiety. For me, that is a trigger to dig deep. Some nights, I fall asleep while praying. Some nights, it is freezing cold or pouring down rain and I will stand outside and worship. I have to go outside because I was not blessed with a singing voice that sounds like angels-I might need to send apology cards to my neighbors. I am far from it. I also enjoy the alone time, just me, God, the stillness of living out in the country and with hands lifted I worship. You guys, I just know that I need God more than ever before. I need Him to be with me all day, every day.

I am thankful to belong to a family of believers who are focused on the hope that comes with having a personal relationship with Jesus. I am thankful for HIS grace and the Freedom that we can experience as a result of grace. I am thankful to be a part of something that words will never adequately describe. I am blown away by how believers come together in the face of a pandemic and pray collaboratively for a loved one. Words cannot begin to explain the gravity of what it feels like when Jesus enters the scene. Lives are being changed. God is not finished. He is moving and working behind the scenes. There is hope. I mean God knows you. He knows what you are going through. He knows your hurts. Press in. Be different. We are called to love others, encourage others and spread the Gospel.

Jesus, I come to you today with a grateful heart. I pray for our world. I pray for our country. I lift up those who are suffering. I am praying for healing. I am praying for believers to go viral with their faith. I am praying hearts, minds, and relationships. Jesus, I am thankful for your unforgiving love and mercy. I will continue to lift you higher and bless your name during the storm and the times of prosperity. I pray that we enter the holiday season with grateful hearts and contentment and peace. Lord, we lay our burdens at your feet. In your loving name me pray.

Jesus, I just want to take this time to thank you for all you do and continue to do. Lord, I am praying for those who do not have a personal relationship with you. Jesus,

I pray that humility creates a pathway for walls to come tumbling down and God's grace to enter hearts and lives begin to change as others accept you into their hearts. I pray that folks find hope through Jesus. I pray that through the acceptance of Jesus, hearts can be mended, and hope is restored. Thank you for being a good, good Father.

CPSIA information can be obtained
at www.ICGtesting.com
Printed in the USA
BVHW041039190122
626618BV00016B/450